HEY, TIGER—
YOU NEED TO MOVE YOUR MARK BACK

HEY, TIGER—
YOU NEED TO MOVE
YOUR MARK BACK

9 SIMPLE WORDS THAT CHANGED
THE GAME OF GOLF FOREVER

STEVE SCOTT
AND
TRIPP BOWDEN

Afterword by Kristi Hommel Scott

Skyhorse Publishing

Skyhorse Publishing books may be purchased in bulk at special discounts for sales promotion, corporate gifts, fund-raising, or educational purposes. Special editions can also be created to specifications. For details, contact the Special Sales Department, Skyhorse Publishing, 307 West 36th Street, 11th Floor, New York, NY 10018 or info@skyhorsepublishing.com.

Skyhorse® and Skyhorse Publishing® are registered trademarks of Skyhorse Publishing, Inc.®, a Delaware corporation.

Visit our website at www.skyhorsepublishing.com.

10 9 8 7 6 5 4 3 2 1

Library of Congress Cataloging-in-Publication Data is available on file.

Cover design by Kai Texel
Cover photo by Gary Hellwege
Back cover photograph credit: Getty Images

ISBN: 978-1-5107-6529-0
Ebook ISBN: 978-1-5107-6530-6

Printed in the United States of America

To the future generation of golfers everywhere, may you always carry forth the honor and traditions of our great game and forever play and compete in the words of the great Nelson Mandela, "Live life as though nobody is watching, and express yourself as though everyone is listening."

"Achievements on the golf course are not what matters, decency and honesty are what matter."
—**Tiger Woods**

Contents

PROLOGUE

IT'S THE SUMMER OF '96, AUGUST 25TH, 5:56 p.m., and the entire world of golf is about to change in the most unpredictable of ways.

Not because of a stroke taken.

But because of a stroke that wasn't.

IT'S THE FINALS OF THE US AMATEUR, the biggest amateur golf tournament in the world, considered a major by many, including the great Bobby Jones (he won five) and equally great Jack Nicklaus (he won two) and, apparently, a young, two-time defending champion Tiger Woods from California, with wings on his swing, who is getting absolutely thrashed by an equally young Steve Scott from Florida, who is much more walk-along-the-ground than wings, and is in a state of disbelief. While certainly quite confident in his own game, Steve didn't see this coming.

Certainly not like this.

Simply dominating Steve off the tee, this amazing Tiger Woods kid flies Steve's drives by 50 yards or more, depending on club choice. When Tiger is hitting wedge into the green, Steve is hitting 5-iron. It's really an unfair fight.

Even Tiger's stinger 2-iron off the tee creeps up too close for comfort to Steve's flushed drives.

Steve and Tiger are polar opposites, both personally and geographically. But they do have this one thing in common.

Both collegians are vying for the US Amateur title and the ultimate stepping-stone to lucrative PGA Tour contracts and the chance to create immortality. Win, and the world is your oyster.

Lose, and you are the discarded shell.

The US Am.

Thirty-six holes define the US Am's final's match, grueling to say the least under Pumpkin Ridge Golf Club's ceaseless summer heat, despite its Pacific Northwest Oregon location. But both of these young guns are young and foolish—they are 19 and 20, after all, and their adrenaline is flowing like a live volcano. This is the biggest moment of their very young lives.

Five thousand, five hundred and thirty-eight entries into the tournament have now become two.

The first 18 holes sees Steve Scott a mind-numbing 5 holes up on Tiger Woods, who has yet to lose a finals match in all his born days, in spite of being 6-down to Tripp Kuehne in '94 and 3-down to Buddy Marucci in '95.

Since embarking on his unthinkable tear through the amateur ranks, Tiger is 35–0 en route to all his previous USGA victories (three straight USGA Junior Ams and two consecutive US Ams), and on this day he is vying for match number 36, for a place in golf history.

This is an absolute butt whooping. Steve should know. He's had one or two in his young 19 years of life, including one from Tiger in the final round of a college tournament hardly nine months prior. Score of 80 for Steve, 70 for Tiger. Ass kicked.

But on this day, Steve Scott is trashing Tiger's perfect script altogether.

Imagine being down 28–3 in the Super Bowl rolling into the fourth quarter, 5-zip in a soccer match midway through, a 20-point lead in basketball with little time left on the clock.

Keep something in mind. In the history of the game of golf, *no one* has ever won three U.S. Amateurs in a row. Not the great Bobby Jones, the equally great Jack Nicklaus, nor the greatest amateur golfer of the modern era (next to the one standing beside Steve on the first tee of the finals match, that is), Jay Sigel.

No one.

Wow.

Tiger changes outfits after the first 18-hole pummeling.

Because Steve was so far ahead, NBC was worried that the finals match might be over far too early for their TV window. There's a long intermission—90 minutes. Almost double a Super Bowl halftime. Is it the longest intermission in US Amateur history?

That is a long time, for someone with momentum, to, well, lose said momentum, and someone else to gain it.

Tiger changes into a red shirt and dark pants, from a morning match of white shirt and khakis.

Steve stays the same. After all, he doesn't want to break the mojo. While Tiger heads to the practice tee with his golf swing coach, the legendary Butch Harmon, and his sports psychologist, Jay Brunza, Steve has lunch with his aunt, uncle, and caddy and then goes shopping in the pro shop, with his girlfriend, Kristi.

Souvenirs of a magical week.

Girlfriend Kristi is also Steve's caddy this magical week, by the way, and she is damn good at what she does. With all the aspects of toting the rock—clubbing your player, talking him off the ledge, keeping him pumped as a jumpy castle or cucumber calm. Kristi is also a fine player in her own right.

Kristi and Steve are like Batman and Robin. How awesome is *that*? You have the love of your life on your bag for the biggest moment of *your* life.

FROM THE FIRST SHOT TIGER HITS ON the practice tee in the practice session with Butch by his side, he starts smiling. And laughing.

Laughing.

Who laughs when you're 5-down in the US Amateur with life-changing history on the line?

The second 18 holes of this historic match at Pumpkin Ridge, like often in the back 9 of our lives, is drastically different. Steve Scott has moments where he leaks oil like a drip pan, while Tiger dials it in like an old rotary phone, no number forgotten, just as Tiger will do just a few months later, when he wins his first PGA Tour event at The Las Vegas Invitational, beating PGA Championship winner Davis Love III in a playoff, one of many playoffs and Tour events Tiger will win over the course of his legendary career.

(Tiger would come into that event finishing 11th, T5, and T3 and ride that momentum like a Cowabunga wave into a historic 12-shots-clear-of-the-field Masters victory the following season. In his first full year on Tour, Tiger wins a Major. Crazy. And yet right now Steve Scott has him on the ropes, like Muhammad Ali on Joe Frazier in the Thrilla in Manila!)

But how about *this* for momentum?

Better yet, a lifetime momentum changer.

Tiger will stride around the Witch Hollow Course at Pumpkin Ridge like a man possessed, hitting twenty-eight of his final twenty-nine greens—think about that for a second—and on the second 18 miraculously gets the finals match two down, with three to play.

After being five down in the morning, Tiger is still, somehow, very, very much alive.

Yet, as soon as Tiger gets close to a miracle in the making, Steve's oil stops leaking, when the University of Florida All-American holes a miracle flop shot from the deep spinach for a birdie two, to win the next hole, the 10th at Pumpkin Ridge, a deceptively difficult par three.

The stars are aligning for young Steve Scott, one by one. Constellations, too. Even the shooting stars are smiling down as they fade away into the night, dotted mayonnaise on a pumpernickel bread sky. Steve's girlfriend, Kristi, whom he will one day marry and raise a happy family with, is on the bag. Could it get any better than this? This is the stuff that only happens on the big screen.

But Tiger has seen that movie before.

And thus, here is where the world of golf changes.

Forever.

The sixteenth green—the 34th hole of the match—at Pumpkin Ridge.

Tiger will soon bury a 6-footer for birdie, after deftly spinning a sand wedge down the slope following a 330-yard drive—yes, he hit it that far off the tee. Then there's Steve, with a breaking 10-footer after a blast out of the bunker—a pretty sweet shot from a very testy lie.

But Tiger's ball mark is in the way—it's in the direct line of Steve's putt. Steve politely asks Tiger to move his mark one to the right, and his opponent politely obliges. After all, golf is a gentlemen's game. Gentlewomen, too.

Steve cans his 10-footer for par like it has eyes, as if the ice water flowing in Tiger's veins now flows through his, too.

Tiger steps in to make his putt for the win. To go 1-down, with two to play, and the match very much alive, unthinkably resuscitated by a 20-year-old kid who will one day go on to lay strong claim as the greatest golfer in the world, and of all time. Lost in the moment, perhaps, or perhaps thinking himself capable of making any putt from any distance without fail—as he has shown his entire life—Tiger doesn't move his mark back.

It bears repeating.

Tiger doesn't move his mark back.

Tiger puts his ball down behind his coin, behind his moved, but not moved *back*, mark. If Tiger putts out from there, as he is just about to do, had Steve said nothing, Tiger loses the hole, the US Amateur, and, up to this point in his young life, everything he's ever dreamed of.

Match over. Place in golf history: poof.

Life forever changed, and Steve Scott wins the US Amateur Championship, lucrative sponsorships, and starts on the PGA Tour that will surely come his way and who knows what else.

Steve Scott's world is about to explode in exponential ways if only he says . . .

Well, nothing.

Stay silent, and Steve is set for life. At this point, Steve is just beginning his journey, jump-started by cables unimaginable. And what a journey it could be, would be.

Should be?

Phil Knight, founder of the all-mighty Nike, watches all

this unfold live and in person, as he is in the gallery, step for step. Phil also has a $40 million contract in his hand, literally, and it doesn't have Steve Scott's name on it. Phil is ready to hand it over to Tiger, with Mont Blanc pen in hand for him to sign on the dotted line, when Tiger wins his third US Amateur in a row.

Something no one has ever done in the history of the sport. If.

If Steve Scott doesn't say these nine selfless words, "Hey, Tiger—You need to move your mark back," *none* of this happens. No Nike contract (at least not one worth $40 million), no US Amateur three-peat, no USGA Championship immortality, no Kilimanjaro mountain-sized level of confidence, no more lack of fear of other players, and dare we say no 80-plus PGA Tour wins, and absolutely no way is his name on 15 major championship trophies.

Even Tiger himself will later say he likely would not have turned pro that day, had he lost.

Had he lost.

None of the above happens if Steve Scott stays silent.

And Tiger loses.

And Steve wins.

And Steve's world changes forever.

And so does Tiger's.

BECAUSE OF STEVE SCOTT'S NINE SELFLESS WORDS, Tiger does indeed move his mark back, albeit without the least bit of acknowledgment to Steve, cans his 6-foot birdie putt, and wins the hole to push the match onward.

And then:

In dizzying, hell-bent-for-leather style, Tiger concludes the comeback of a lifetime (it really was epic; there is no denying that), draining an improbable 40-footer for birdie to square the match on the 17th hole, the match's 35th. Shortly thereafter, (man, it happened so quick), Tiger officially wins his third US Amateur in a row—sealing the deal in a sudden-death playoff on the 38th hole, when Steve lips out a seven-footer and Tiger taps in from two—and the world of golf changes.

Forever. Just like that.

But Steve Scott said those words.

As life-changing as childbirth.

Steve could have stopped Tiger from winning the biggest golf tournament in both of their young lives, if the golf gods were to guess, had he stayed silent. But to stay silent would not be golf, would not be the way the game was meant to be played, the way Steve was taught growing up by his father and an unassuming local Florida golf pro named Ray.

Honesty, integrity, truth, kindness. Respect for one another. Respect for the game. Respect for the moment. Respect for, well, everything. The thought of staying silent never even crossed Steve's mind.

I should know.

I am Steve Scott, and this is my story.

But don't feel bad for me. Please. Yes, losing in the finals of the '96 US Amateur to Tiger Woods, when he was trying to make history, ripped my heart out, vena cava to valve.

How could it not?

But I'm okay with it. At the end of this story, I hope you are, too. After all, my life turned out better than I could ever have imagined. So did Tiger's.

I guess it was meant to be, you know? I played the role I was meant to play. And I'm okay with that, too.

Let me tell you how it all went down. It's a mighty fun ride, in spite of the ending on that magical August day.

Oddly enough, that ending was just the beginning.

1

ENTRY

My earliest memory of the game of golf is simple, kinda like me.

It all started in the kitchen, at my parents' house, with a big plastic club, a putting cup, and a giant plastic golf ball, big as a grapefruit.

Our kitchen is a runway kitchen—long and skinny. I think the proper term is a galley kitchen, like on a ship or something, but of course I don't know this at the time. I'm three years old, in 1980. I loved to just whack that golf ball down the kitchen. And somehow try to find that putting cup.

My dad cut down a putter for me later in life, age five, I think it was. I'm really short for my age, with blue eyes, and my brown hair is cut into a "Buster Brown" type of mop (Mom's choice). It's an interesting look, but I don't have a horse in the race. I can vote, for sure, but it won't count.

This cut-down putter is my first real golf club, and it feels electric in my hands. It's like something from a Putt-Putt course, looking back on it, but it boasts a real metal head—a rectangular piece of metal that jutted out from the shaft from the heel. It wasn't Ben Crenshaw's baby—no 8802 by any stretch.

But, man, I loved that thing.

I still have it in my attic, somewhere, along with other memories.

Attics are full of memories—many forgotten, until you climb up the ladder and go up there and put your hands on them. And then the waves pass over you like the highest of tides, when the perigee moon is big and full and screaming of gravity.

My brother, Roger, is five-and-a-half years older than me, and when I was five, we had a brilliant idea. We decided to put real golf balls, beat-up range balls I think they were, on top of sprinkler heads and whack 'em down the street with our putters. Not even real clubs. Seventy, eighty yards or more. With real golf balls. In our neighborhood!

It was the dumbest thing, looking back on it. But we didn't break a window, didn't dent a car. Still, I can't believe we did that. Fifty, seventy yards down the street. Boy, would that golf ball bounce!

That was pretty nuts. But, man, was it fun.

I got my first set of clubs from my grandmother, on my dad's side of the family. Her name was Frances Scott. She had played golf a long time before me—and had this old-school set of Patty Berg clubs. Wilson's, I think they were. Leather grips, with the reminder. They weren't even round. An angled part—a dent almost, to show you where to angle your forefingers.

I think I was seven. Nothing fit me at all. But I couldn't help taking a liking to the game. My dad played, and I recall many great times on various public courses with him. The only time I was ever a member of a private club was back then, as well: Inveraray, where they used to host the Jackie Gleason Classic PGA tournament. Just for a couple of years. Between the ages of eleven and thirteen. And then, well, my parents got divorced. That sucked. And I moved to Arkansas. My time of playing golf at a private club was very brief.

I didn't grow up with a silver spoon in my mouth. But when it came to the game of golf, I guess you could say I grew up with a ladle.

Plastic, of course.

Just like the golf ball I chased down our galley kitchen.

MY BROTHER ROGER HAS ALWAYS BEEN A much better athlete than me and bigger, too. He even became a football kicker in high school—Roger could kick it for miles—but the game of golf didn't entice him so much. He didn't have the patience for it. But we had a bunch of fun with it, goofing about.

For a little while, anyway.

During the summers in South Florida, Roger and I would go around and play the local courses, with the American Lung Card, which my dad had bought for us. Roger opted out more often than not, so often it ended up being me and my dad. But I understood why, even though I missed him being out there with me.

It is *so*, so hot in South Florida. You can't walk to your mailbox without sweating like a sinner in church. It's *that* hot. And every afternoon, around 2 o'clock, there is a thunderstorm.

Like the sky has had enough, and it needs to explode.

It's funny how different two boys who grow up under the same roof can turn out. Roger is a trainer now—a sports and conditioning specialist who trains the Chinese Olympic speed skaters. A heck of an athlete, Roger is, but he pretty much just didn't have the patience for the game of golf. He played one tournament in his life, I think, and hated it. He never loved the game like I did—it didn't move fast enough for him. Roger likes to rock and roll. Let's go, Steve, let's go!

But that's cool.

I'm mighty proud of him, my brother.

I'M GOING TO BACK UP A SECOND if that's okay with you.

Man, I loved the challenge of hitting those Patty Bergs. Blades, knives, with no forgiveness whatsoever. What you hit is what you get. Polar opposite of today's equipment. I would later get a set of mishmash clubs—but the Patty Bergs is how I learned the game. Kind of akin to Sam Snead and his hickory stick in the deep woods of Virginia, hitting pinecones.

And by hickory stick, I mean it was a stick of hickory.

Well, along came the Lung Card, breathing new life into me. Where I could play all these great courses that we could not have afforded otherwise, at a greatly discounted fee. And I would spend all day there on those courses. I would chip, and putt, find someone to play with.

Boca Raton was busy as a Christmas Walmart in the winter, but a ghost town in the summer, because it was so darn hot. There was a place called Boca West—oddly enough, a track where I would some eight years later shoot 64 in the final round to qualify for the US PGA Junior. Funny, how life comes full circle. There was a place in Georgia, too—Callaway Gardens. Our one big family vacation in the summer.

Man, they had a lot of golf there. Mountain View, Lake View, Garden View—which was kind of like an executive course, comprised of half par-threes and half par-fours.

So much fun to play.

I was in Heaven.

My dad would sometimes play a place in Tamarac, Florida, a couple cities away from where we lived in Coral Springs, a place called Colony West. They had a big 18-hole course—a proper one. I'm eight or nine or something. It's a Saturday morning. Across the street was their executive course. Cost five bucks. That's where Roger and I would play, paired up with random people. Mom never played. She's more into acting and drama, stuff like that, like my daughter, which I think is pretty awesome.

It's funny, how life skips a generation.

IN FEBRUARY OF '88, I'M LOST LIKE most kids, but curious, too. It was then that I meet a guy named Ray Daley, near Pompano Beach, at a place called Crystal Lake Country Club—a public track. And by public, I mean come one, come all, from wherever you may be. Which I thought was great—that's how *I* got to go there.

I am as public as they come.

Ray is maybe 75 at the time. Gray mustache. Rocking the Sansabelt pants, V-cut at the bottom, to complement his blue golf shirt, with the double-button pocket and the bat-wing collar. And he is just so nice. Felt like I had known Ray all my life, just from the way he welcomed me into his world, the world of golf.

Ray—he played on the PGA Tour, back in the '40s. Not sure if he ever won anything—kinda sort of unknown out there on the Tour, but he was some kind of special to me. Someone like that doesn't come along often in life.

Ray was tremendous.

I'm not telling this story without him.

I meet Ray at a golf show in Fort Lauderdale, Florida. Bunch of vendors, hitting nets, check this out, check that out, try this, try that, pull out your wallet—that kinda thing. And this gentleman comes over, this Ray fellow, with gray hair, gray mustache, the outfit, like I said, and looks at a couple of my swings. I felt instantly comfortable in his presence, like Winnie the Pooh and Piglet. To this day, I never knew why Ray came over. Why Ray picked me. I guess he liked what he saw? Or maybe thought what he would one day see?

I honestly don't know.

Ray walks over, talks to me about me about my grip. And how it has to change. From ten-finger like a baseball bat to, well, something else entirely.

The Vardon Grip.

Holy moly.

That's a big ol' change. In golf, your grip is like your personality. At that time, ten fingers *was* my personality.

Ray is the one who convinced me to go to the Vardon grip, the overlap grip, where you tuck your left index finger above the pinky finger of your right and you marry them. Two become one. For some reason I trusted this Ray fellow, this perfect stranger that I meet at a golf show in Fort Lauderdale, Florida, who would later become my golf mentor and dear friend, and I never looked back.

After I hit a few more shots with my newfound Vardon grip, Ray says to my dad, "Hey, why don't you two come down to Crystal Lake Saturday morning? At 9 o'clock. I'd like to give Steve a proper lesson."

I will always remember it was a Saturday morning. I love

the weekends. So, I was all in. And I am as excited as all get out.

We go there, my dad and I, and Ray's Crystal Lake place is a basic driving range, about as raw as you get, but I'm hitting off a mat, which is easy to hit off of. Like hitting off a sponge, kinda—gives you confidence you might not have discovered otherwise. Kinda like teeing up a sand wedge to learn the game before you rip a driver.

Ray's driving range is small. No grass to speak of. Not a lot of land, either. Seems to stretch out forever, though, in reverse, odd as that may sound.

Like it is in front of me and behind me, all at the same time.

I never take a lesson off grass with Ray. The balls on his range were limited-flight balls—they felt like hitting rubber, kinda like hitting a superball you get out of a gumball machine after you put in a quarter and you get what you get. They were yellowed, old, and scratched up, like an old tomcat. They have the paint on them, too—the painted red stripes that define the middle of the ball. I'll never forget it. There's a net on the other side of the range, a few stories high, but I can't hit it far enough to reach.

Ray gives me a 30-minute lesson my first time with him, and it is the lesson of my life.

I will never forget the paint. Nor the lesson.

Ray tells me to "put it parallel," with the leading edge of the ball, I mean, with the clubface, because if I hit the paint, it will get all over my clubs.

Ray often said I had a lateral shift into the ball, which I guess you would call a lurch. Ray would say: *"Steve, you're lurching too much."* I'm still not entirely sure what that means, but

Ray's words did teach me to stay still and to swing more like a pendulum than a kindergarten swing set, the two-seater kind that rock back and forth off their foundation if you get going too fast.

Ray got me out of the big-time lateral shifts and taught me a bunch of shots, too. Draw it this way, fade it that way—not that I could ever actually hit a fade. Hit me one low, Steve; hit me one high—now *that* I could do. Ray says all day long to me: hip and hand, together, Steve; hip and hand together. That was Ray's swing key for me.

"Chase your hands to your hips, Steve," Ray would say.

The hip and the hand should get to impact at the same time. Try that sometime. It will blow your mind how well it works. Chase your hands to your hips. Hard as hell to do, but it works like magic.

Especially when you are struggling.

THERE WAS THIS CRAZY-TALL WOODEN POLE—an electricity pole, like a big, wooden pretzel rod—standing in the middle of the range. Thick wires came off it like rabid cables. I had to hit a big 7-iron out to it at the time to reach. It was 70 feet tall? Maybe more. But when you're small, everything seems big. Maybe 120 yards out or so, that pole was, from where I was hitting off those cushy mats, and I remember trying to hit that pole on the fly because Ray told me to. I'm hitting from an elevated tee. Hip and hand together. And I did hit that pole, once or twice.

Hip and hand together. Chasing, like you do your dreams.

Chase your hands to your hips, Steve. The hip and the hand should get to impact at the same time, so they become one, like a marriage.

Blind squirrel finding an acorn, that was me—a blind squirrel, hitting a draw, but Ray was one heck of a walking stick. It was the cool satisfaction of learning the game, from Ray and the way he taught me, I guess you could say, that made me fall in love with golf.

Suddenly, I could see.

Thank you, Ray. I can never thank you enough.

I remember my dad asking, funny enough, at the end of the first lesson, as he shook Ray's hand and thanked him: "Please, tell me—what do we owe you?"

And Ray says, "Nothing. You don't owe me nothing." And then Ray kneels down to get eye level with me and looks me in the eyes like *Star Wars* radars and says, "Go and love and play the game like a kid, kid."

Ray Daley, the only golf teacher I ever had as a youngster, never once charged me for a lesson. *Ever.* Think about that for a second. We could have paid him his going rate—60 dollars an hour. It would've made things tight at home, but we could have paid it.

I GOT THE NEWS WHEN I WAS fourteen years old that Ray had passed away. I cried like a baby when I heard. My heart changed that day. People like Ray aren't meant to die.

I think about Ray often.

Pretty much every day of my life.

2

AWAKENING, IN REVERSE

I PLAY FOR RAY.

Ray taught me how to love the game, and how to hit that pole, electric as an eel, and *Man, hit it on the fly, Steve. Come on kid, I know you can do it.*

Ray gave me the belief I could do that. Ray gave me the belief that I could do anything.

MY PARENTS' DIVORCE IN THE EARLY PART of 1989 kinda rocks my world—not like the Scorpions' *Hurricane*, but certainly a proper summer storm, and my mom remarries.

My parents' divorce becomes a catalyst for me working on my golf game, like a kid possessed. I'm as wrecked as a train falling off the tracks and crashing into the mountain, not getting up to the top and circling around like in the movie *The Polar Express*, where all those kids are laughing and loving and wondering what's coming next. I'm not laughing and wondering about anything but fear and the unknown.

I am an absolute mess.

But golf becomes my best friend. I want to become great, to tell the game of golf: thank you, for saving me. That's how I'm channeling my energy and frustrations and the sadness that I'm feeling. I know things aren't right at home—not even sure where home is right now—and I'm trying to find an outlet. Find a way to fix it, whatever *it* is.

I've got to escape and find me again. This sadness has to escape and find happiness again. I am so lost it's not funny. Well, of course, it *is* funny. You have to find humor in sadness, otherwise you've got nothing.

Golf becomes my outlet, and I plug in like nothing you've ever seen.

My broken-home therapy sessions—please know none of this is on my mom or dad: things just didn't work out, life happens, and I love them both like crazy to this day—come in the form of lengthy putting sessions at a place called Prairie Creek Country Club (oftentimes the only thing country about such places is the surroundings, for the record, which is just fine with me), an ordinary, run-of-the-mill public track near my new house in Rogers, in the northwest part of Arkansas. Prairie Creek is the first time I ever putt on bent-grass greens, and they are so much smoother than the Bermuda greens I am used to. It's like putting on a tortilla as opposed to a taco. Some of these sessions make their way onto the actual golf course, with strangers, folks I meet for the first time and often the last.

My mom and stepdad don't play golf at all—so it's just me and the fence post, and these random strangers who become acquaintances.

The best thing about this time at the course is that I am in control of my life for the first time ever. It's just me and the golf ball, and I soon find that I am usually pretty good in control of that little, white, dimpled thing, which at the time is exactly what I needed.

Funny, how something so small can heal a wound so big.

In a sort of backward way, my parents' divorce was one of the best things, if not *the* best, that ever happened to me, sad and terrible as that may sound. Or maybe happy. My parents' divorce brought me closer to golf than I ever would have been otherwise, and it drove me to become better each and every day and to want to one day be an American golfing bad mamajama. By that, I just mean a pretty good player and, well, maybe win the Masters.

Well, there's that.

I don't blame my parents for parting ways. Sometimes, things just don't work out. But their marriage gave me life, and later, new life, and I will forever be grateful for that.

Thank you, Mom and Dad.

3
DEPARTURE

I AM TWELVE YEARS OLD AND IN the 8th grade, a tough time to be a kid, especially when you are as lost as I am. Off I have gone from South Florida to the northwest corner of Arkansas, with my mom and her new husband and my grandma, to this city called Rogers. What kind of city would be named after my brother? I can't help but wonder, and I am oddly excited to see why, yet equally excited to stay put.

I also want to crawl in a hole and die.

I know absolutely no one here, in this Rogers town, and my only friend is golf. I keep it that way for the longest time, flying solo. I could have turned to drugs or alcohol, or who knows what else, lost and lonely as I was, but I turned to golf.

I am a 12-year-old train wreck, but I'm finding my way back onto the tracks, thanks to golf.

THERE IS MORE. THERE IS ALWAYS MORE. Not saying that's a bad thing. Often, it's good. In the long run, I mean.

My stepfather loses his job at the radio station in Arkansas and gets a new one in Memphis, Tennessee, so off I go again, midway through my 8th-grade year, away from my new normal. Another year of going into a moment where you know absolutely no one.

Awkward, to say the least.

I do have a cool memory of Memphis, however—it's not Memphis's fault I got uprooted for the second time in my life and planted like one of those sickly city oak trees in the median of a downtown street. There is a golf pro there, at the local track, the Plantation I think it's called.

His name is Bill Munguia. They call him Goose. He's really, really good to me. Takes me under his wing—kinda funny, considering his nickname.

Bill was a goose with one heck of a wingspan.

I break 70 there for the first time at the ripe old age of twelve. At Goose's course, The Plantation in Olive Branch, Mississippi, just south of the Memphis, Tennessee, state line. Public track. Goose lets me play there for free, just like Ray did, with his lessons. I still have the scorecard somewhere—attic or maybe in my back pocket.

Four under. 68.

Sixty-eight! Monumental in a kid's head. The week before I was 4-under, and then went bogey, double bogey, and double and shot 73.

But I'm gonna back up for just a bit, if you don't mind. I will do this time and again in our story—I hope that's okay.

People my age didn't really play golf, back in my day. So I always played with older folks. That's who I learned from. From observation. There wasn't really anyone to look up to.

I learned both what *not* to do, and what *to* do, from observation.

Golf just wasn't a cool sport, back then in the late 1980s, for a 12-year-old kid, even though it was damn cool for me. That said—you are not getting the chicks playing golf (although I ultimately got mine—I love you, Kristi!). But that wasn't what I loved, and still love, about the game.

I loved the challenge of challenging yourself—say that twice while chewing gum and walking backward. The challenge of beating your best score, on a hole, for the round, you name it.

Still do.

4
THE BEST TEACHER
IS YOURSELF

I ONCE HEARD THAT THE BEST TEACHER is yourself—once you get a proper foundation under you, of course—and was once asked if I believed that. I do. Completely. Wholeheartedly.

I'm mostly self-taught, once Ray taught me how to teach myself—certainly once I moved away to Memphis, and away from Ray. There were no cell phones back then, and we couldn't really afford a flood of long-distance phone calls. I figured it out myself, although I missed Ray terribly. He was the pat on my back, the hand on my shoulder when I needed the reassurance you can only get through human contact.

I had to. Be self-taught after Ray, I mean. I didn't have the most orthodox setup, wasn't winning any awards as the poster boy for a textbook setup, stance, and alignment, but I knew what I had to do to make sure my golf ball curved from right to left every time it left my club. Aim to the right, with a lot of hand and forearm rotation through the shot. I knew where the target was, and I visualized the shot before I hit it. And the more I practiced, be it bunker shots, irons, driver, woods, rolling putts, hitting flop shots, or tying your shoes in the parking lot, I just kept honing in. *My* in. But I'm not sure I could tell you how I did what I did. Not back then, anyway. I had golf friends who got lessons from this famous teacher, that famous teacher, fancy country clubs.

We were unconditional friends on the golf course, but we ran with different crowds once we putted out on eighteen.

I never had that. Their world. But that's cool. Life is life.

I knew I could play a draw, and I did, and I built my game around a "spinny" golf ball—sadly, the modern golf ball doesn't allow that—another story for another time.

I'll never forget my first summer of playing in the Broward County Junior Golf Association, and they always ran a slate of events in South Florida at local courses around the county. I'm ten years old, and they put me in the D Flight—D as in you Don't Stand a Chance, which is five tee boxes away from the first tee and you play from the red tees, add up your score, and low score wins, at Inveraray Country Club.

I remember telling my mom and dad: "I'm gonna win this thing."

I just knew I was going to win.

I didn't win.

Two events later, at a place called Broken Woods Country Club (how's *that* for a name, and how fitting for me, at the time and maybe later), I shoot 19 for five holes. Couple par 3s, the rest par 4s. And I win the event. From the red tees! The D Flight, the third tournament I ever played in my life.

It's the summer of '87.

The competitive fire was burning in me like an inferno, and it never went out. You could say God gave it to me. I certainly never knew life without it.

No one ever taught me that competitive fire, though Ray certainly ignited it with his unorthodox aim-'n'-flame and a telephone pole covered in lighter fluid. I just go out and hit it and I think: I've gotta beat you. That's all there is to it.

I've thought that way since I first whacked that plastic putter and ball down our galley kitchen eight years ago. Maybe that is why I thought I could beat the great Tiger Woods, some ten years later.

I grew up believing I could beat anybody.

5
ME, AGAIN, FOR WHAT IT'S WORTH
A LITTLE BACK STORY

I THINK, MAYBE, I WAS COCKY OR brash, or whatever the case may be. Inwardly, inner—I still am. But you learn over time that it's not socially acceptable to go around and tell everybody you're gonna win, that you are gonna kick their butt, no matter what, come hell or high water. But that drive within me will always be there.

It's in my DNA. It's just in me.

I can't help it. Born with it, I guess, like you're born with the color of your hair, or the gait of your walk.

On my honeymoon, with Kristi, I almost get divorced the next day. We were playing tennis, and I was serving too hard. And Kristi didn't like that. We met on a golf course—Kristi is athletically inclined, quite a player in her own right. But I was trying too hard—trying to win too much. We agreed to tie. She more so than me. Ha!

That was a hard thing for me to do. To bow down in a competition, even if it was to my brand-new, beautiful wife who's also my best friend. But—learning the errors of your ways, it takes time.

In fact, I am still learning.

Honey, I apologize.

6

FAST-FORWARD

I AM FRESH OUT OF HIGH SCHOOL and have qualified for my first US Amateur on my first try. I'm also on my way to the University of Florida, as a freshman, to play golf and represent the college. A full-ride scholarship, books paid for, dorm room, food, too—the whole nine. I have saved my parents a bunch of money.

I am also scared half to death.

I'm also about to lose in the semifinals in the next ten minutes, to the great amateur golfer Buddy Marucci, at Newport Country Club, in Newport, Rhode Island.

Buddy is a badass.

My life is moving so, so fast. And Buddy is so, so good. Man, can he putt like nobody's business. Buddy wields the flat stick like a Jedi (and by that I mean Jedi Luke Skywalker in the *Mandalorian* episode) with a light saber—I kid you not.

Had I beaten Buddy in that semifinals match, my finals match opponent would have been, of all people, Tiger Woods.

God has a great sense of humor.

The year is 1995. I have no way of knowing, but the negative of losing to Buddy will set so much positive stuff in my life in motion.

Kristi, the bride I almost got divorced from via hitting a tennis ball too hard into her breadbasket during a friendly honeymoon match (I thought it a friendly—my bride not so much—rookie mistake) caddied for me in the qualifier for that '95 US Am.

Kristi and I started dating seriously on November 26, the year prior.

One of the best days of my life.

THE US AMATEUR IS A 36-HOLE QUALIFIER. Mid-July, I think it was. Kristi and I had both just graduated high school. The top two or three players only out of maybe 70 to 80 players per qualifier location make it, but I believe it's worth a roll of the dice. Why not? Place called Quail Ridge Country Club in Boynton Beach, Florida. Kristi played high-school golf, college, too, so she has game and has beaten me on a couple occasions.

Funny, the things you remember.

Anyway, it's raining like Noah's Ark during the qualifier. Symbolic, I guess, since Kristi and I are walking two by two. But I somehow shoot 3-under on the second day, olive branch in hand, and make it to the '95 US Amateur in Rhode Island, with Kristi on my bag. There are some times, some moments, when I'm struggling during the qualifier, kinda like in any round you play—searching for this, searching for that. And it's funny how I've always, when I've struggled, tried to picture the swings of golfers I really liked. Nick Price, Hale Irwin—very upright, tight turns. I would try to mentally turn into those players. Those were my swing thoughts. And the moments when I was struggling over those 36 holes, Kristi says to me, "Hey, why don't you swing like Nick Price on this one? I know how you like to duplicate swings."

And lo and behold I hit a great iron shot and make birdie after a bogey.

Kristi is great, and I mean great, with the mental part of the game. She can tap into my mental game, my psyche, like nobody's business. She was so, so good at doing just that at Quail Ridge. Still is. She was like my sports psychologist out there, whatever that means, since I've never had one before. But Kristi can calm the storm long before the waves or rain or howling winds hit my head and crash into my brain.

So.

I just pictured Nick Price swinging the golf club as only he can, quick yet even tempo, maybe the best follow-through in recent memory, and off I went. And that gets me through, and I end up winning the qualifier.

Unfortunately, money, or lack thereof, doesn't allow Kristi to make her way up to Newport CC to be on the bag for me, though she does surprise me on the back 9 of the semifinals thanks to the kindness of her sister and my brother-in-law, who drove her seven-plus hours north up the hill so she could catch me on number 10 of my semifinals match with the great Buddy Marucci.

Kristi was simply incredible at Quail Ridge. No way do I qualify for the US Amateur in Rhode Island without Kristi by my side. I hope I have thanked her more than once for that, over the passing years.

7

AN ENLIGHTENING THAT GOES DARK

I ROLL INTO NEWPORT A COCKY KID, thinking I'm gonna blow the world up.

I come out the first day, playing what they call the secondary stroke course site—there's always two courses you play for the US Amateur stroke-play qualifier—and this was Wanumetonomy Country Club, a really short golf course with fast, sloping greens. I play a practice round, kinda dig the track; it fits my game, because it's different, like me. It's a different cut of cloth. And I shoot 67 on the first day of stroke-play qualifying.

At eighteen years old.

I'm leading the stroke-play qualifier of the US Amateur after day one. Leading it! Over all of these great players. All American collegians, Mid Amateurs. And me, the punk kid.

The next day at Newport Country Club, I go off on the back 9 first. I shoot one over par, 36—it's a par of 70 at both courses. I'm still in cruise control, though I don't know where

I am, relative to the lead. But I know I'm in pretty good shape. This is a mighty tough track. Par is a very good score here.

As I walk across the putting green toward the first tee, I pass a friend, and he asks how I'm doing. I remember being so cocky, I tell him, "As long as I just keep standing on my own two feet, I'm gonna make this thing."

What a jackass thing to say.

Looking back some 25 years later, I'm still not proud of that. I still would have said it, though. Because that's how much I believed in myself. You gotta believe in yourself, even when you lose.

Otherwise, you've got nothing.

I get out there on the back 9 at Newport, the wind whipping like Indiana Jones's favorite weapon, and the greens getting burnt-toast-crusty and slicker than left-out butter. I start choking my guts out, no idea as to why. I come into the last hole, needing bogey to make it to match play. By a shot. I'm five over on the back 9, now six over for the day.

The last hole at Newport is a dogleg right, maybe 430 yards. I hit it into the fairway bunker, into a crappy lie. I pitch it out and then miss the green with my third shot. Chip it up to eight feet. Somehow, I make the putt, the golf course a blur, the moment out of focus.

Eight feet for bogey.

God made that putt, not me.

I make match play by a shot. Shooting 67–77. The next year, 1996, it will be 79–66, one of the biggest stroke play turnarounds in US Amateur history, coming from out of nowhere—I believe after the 79 I was tied for 242nd out of 312 players—to qualify for match play, seeded in the bottom right-hand bracket.

But at least I'll be seeded with a chance to grow.

If I miss that bogey putt on 18, I'm in a twenty-one-person playoff for two slots. An almost impossible hill to climb. You are not gonna make it through that, barring a miracle, or a boatload of good luck on your end and a boatload of bad luck on theirs.

When I was hot, I was the bonfire from the movie *Grease*. All the high school kids gathered round, John Travolta included. When I was cold, I was your favorite popsicle, straight out the wrapper, so cold it hurt your teeth to bite into it. That was and still is my golf game, although nowadays the hot is a medium flame, like an indirect heat on your grill, and the cold is like a South Florida winter.

A popsicle or a bonfire. That is me.

I don't know how to put a tourniquet on it.

NEWPORT COUNTRY CLUB, RHODE ISLAND. THIS MAY never happen again, but I'd like to throw it out. As a high school kid playing in the US Amateur, I never once played against a collegiate and certainly not a fellow high school kid—I believe I was the only one—in the '95 US Am. Only Mid Am players. I played against five Mid Am gents in a row, guys in their mid-to-late 20s and beyond. Established amateurs with proper credentials. Not sure if that's ever been done before.

Not sure if it matters, though.

There was a guy named Mark Plummer, from Maine, who favored (quite strongly) Yosemite Sam. Mark had a golf swing that looked like it was built out of a phone booth. It was God-awful, but man did Mark make it work. He played Tiger in the semifinals, I think. Before Tiger got to me, and me to him, one year later.

I lose to Buddy Marucci in the semis myself, on the 19th hole. I had a chance to beat Buddy, put the match away. I'm one up with two to play. Drove it into the rough on 17 and blasted my approach—short-sided my approach, actually—and didn't get it up and down. But then I made a huge clutch putt on 18, a downhill left-to-right slider that was faster than a Bugatti, to send it into extra holes.

But Buddy got it up and down on a reachable par 5 from the greenside bunker on the 19th hole. Buddy is just that good—hats off to him. And I missed my eight-foot putt for birdie to tie him. Man, can that guy roll the flat stick.

You have got to give credit where credit is due.

And that was it. I was done. Birdie beats par. But, anyway, that was what I was up against. And I lost.

Damn.

I'll see Buddy in the quarterfinals next year, 1996, and the outcome will be very, very different. I'll be 1-down, with two to play, and win the final two holes to win the match. They say revenge is a dish best served cold, though I wouldn't call taking Buddy down in the quarterfinals in '96 revenge, and/or cold.

Man, it was hot out there.

No, I'd call it learning from experience, learning from the situation.

You gotta *lose*, to learn how to win.

Simple as that.

8

THE 1996 US AMATEUR AT PUMPKIN RIDGE

NORTH PLAINS, OREGON

THE BIGGEST WEEK OF MY YOUNG GOLFING life begins. And ends. All at the same time. I didn't know it then, but this moment in time will hold that auspicious title until they put me in the ground.

At Pumpkin Ridge, much akin to Newport, three of the six matches I play are against Mid Amateurs, giving me eight out of eleven matches against Mid Amateurs. Much older and more experienced players than me.

My first match, however, is against a fellow named Clint Jensen, a collegian like me, and a darn good player in his own right who will go on to marry Lisa Penske, of the Penske Auto family. I think Clint has his moments of glory in sports later in life, but it just doesn't quite work out, and he goes on to do other things. I can dig that.

Ours will be the closest match I play until close becomes no cigar in my finals match against Tiger, and me with a book of matches still in my pocket, ready to strike one so bad I can't see straight.

Clint and I are even in our match going into the par-4 17th. I hit 7-iron to about seven feet. The pin's in a perfect position for my home-grown shot shape—the controlled, soft draw. Buttery, like you could put it on toast.

I make, Clint misses, and we head to the 18th tee with me 1-up and licking my chops, feeling so good, riding on a cloud of confidence like Aladdin on his magic carpet. This match, like the other five I will play this week, feels like destiny. I wish I could bottle why, but I *can* say there's some truth to the old adage "You know when you know."

I knew.

On 18, I play a good hole, perfect drive, and nice shot in, but I miss my birdie putt, and Clint knocks it in close and makes his putt to push that match to extra holes. Hats off to Clint. He made a clutch putt, no doubt.

Playoff, and winner takes all and advances like hope springs eternal.

On the first playoff hole, Clint hits it into the rough, and I stripe one a good 280—heart of the fairway. But I end up missing the green and so does Clint. He has a 15-footer for par after his chip, and I have maybe a 12-footer for par after mine, to win the match and go on, should Clint miss.

Clint misses.

It's the weirdest thing, actually. But sometimes there is a need for out-of-the-blue change.

Because of Clint's miss, I have a 12-footer to win the match and go on to, well, what? Greatness? Give 'em hell, Rydell?

Match number one is mine for the taking if I can hole this 12-footer.

But it is like I am frozen in time.

Remember how Nick Price used to putt? And probably still putts? And oddly enough the way my college coach, Buddy Alexander, used to putt. They both put the putter ahead of the head of the ball prior to the stroke. And then they raise the putter over the ball and *then* they start their stroke. Pretty rare. I only know of two.

Those two.

For whatever reason, and I can't tell you why I did it on that particular putt, but that was my routine on that putt, and I remember it clear as day. The sky cloudless and blue as a robin's egg.

Hmm.

I'm reaching, maybe, but I think what that does is it helps you feel the putter face and where the squareness should be postimpact. I also think it's kinda crazy, but I do it anyway.

I put my putter ahead of the ball, raise it back, and I stroke the putt and bury it.

I win the match on the 19th hole.

Can't tell you why I did it, the change-in-routine putting thing. It was the only time I did it that week or ever again—before or after in my entire golfing life. But it was like something or someone called me to do it.

Otherwise, I would have missed.

I make that putt to win, and so does Tiger, in similar fashion. In his first-round match, not too far removed from mine. Not that I am paying any attention to him, nor him to me.

Neither of us is on the other's radar.

9

A NUMBERS GAME: SUNRISE BEGINS

FROM THE ROUND OF 64 TO THE ROUND OF 32

THERE ARE 5,538 PLAYERS WHO TRY TO qualify for the US Amateur in '96. And yet I am but *one* of them to make it to the round of 32. Humbling to say the least.

My second match is against a Mid-Amateur gent named John Harris, who won the US Amateur in 1993 over Danny Ellis at Champions. John is just three years removed from holding up the winner's trophy, so no question he still has game, and lots of it. In fact, John will join me on the '97 Walker team, going so far as to win us the final point against GB&I, clinching the Cup at Quaker Ridge Golf Club in New York. Man, what a celebration we had!

Funny, how life comes full circle.

John is very much a professional-looking player who just happens to be an amateur. He is very calculating, very even-mannered, a great ball strilker, and always in play. He doesn't get too overly happy when he wins a hole, doesn't get too down when he loses one.

You could learn a lot about internal game management from John Harris.

John is also a member of Augusta National, a little factoid that is not lost on me, and here's why.

The winner of the US Amateur gets an invitation to play in the Masters Tournament the following year. So does the runner-up. Wonder what it must have felt like for John to play in the Masters Tournament as a contestant *and* a member? And I wonder if that has ever happened before. If John and I weren't playing a match to see who advances to the Sweet 16 of the '96 US Amateur, I probably would have asked him.

The odds of being where I am, of being in this situation, are astronomical. Of the more than 5,000 people who are vying to qualify for the US Amateur all over America, only 312 players make it to the stroke-play portion of the tournament, just 6.24 percent of the original number of entries, and of those 312 players, only 64 make it into match play. So, only about 20 percent of the field makes it into match play. The odds, the percentages of making it to the 36-hole finals match, becoming one of just two players at the end when you began as one of 5,538 players—we all start into this as equals—whittled down to 312 and then to 64?

That is only 0.03611 percent! Only getting struck by lightning has a lower percentage.

And to think Tiger will do it three times in a row.

Three times in a row.

"Astronomical" might not be the right word.

In 1990, when Phil Mickelson won, there were 4,765

entries; in '92, when Justin Leonard won, there were roughly 5,700 entries. Next year 5,600, then 5,100. And the year after '96, there were 6,666 entries. Over 1,100 more entries the year after Tiger pulls off the US Amateur trifecta over me.

In 1999, there are almost *8,000* entries.

The Tiger Effect, in full force. There is nothing like it in the world of sport.

In the world in general.

JOHN HARRIS IS ONE HELL OF A player in his own right and standing cinder-block-wall solid in my way of my own destiny, just as I am standing in the way of his. John has won this baby before, and very much believing he can win it again.

John misses a short putt early in our match, even though he is an excellent putter, on the 4th hole, and it takes me by surprise, bit of a shock actually, especially coming from a player of his experience and skill set.

I am guessing it surprised John, too.

It also gets more than just my attention.

Putting always determines the champion—I don't care how well you can hit the golf ball tee to green—if you can't putt, you can't play. Simple as that.

In match play, especially.

When your opponent misses a short putt, it just frees you up. Makes you think, better yet makes you *know*; hey, he's probably gonna miss another one. And he more often than not does.

The putt John misses is just a touch under three feet. It's a putt I almost could've given him, but I didn't. That miss sets the tone of the match early. Whether that early miss got in John's head I'll never really know, but there was no doubt John's putting that day was not up to his (understandably so) lofty standards. When I bury a few early, the pressure falls heavily on John's flat stick, and we all know putting all day under heavy pressure in high-level competition can weigh you down like a diving bell, and you the butterfly.

Putting pressure on your opponent is what match play is all about. You've got to know when to strike, know when to play smart, let them make the first mistake, and when they do, put it in overdrive. You've got to let them know, got to show them that "Hey, I ain't going anywhere. I'm not going to back down. You're gonna have to play your ass off today if you want to have a chance to take me down."

When you have the tee, you have got to put it in the fairway. If it's a par three, you've got to put it on the green. You have got to keep the pressure on. There is no substitute. Simple as that.

It's funny, but it seems like in every match I make more putts than I do in stroke play. I'm much less nervous—it's not even close, actually, in my nervousness—and I hit some miraculous shots that I wouldn't normally hit.

The shot that sticks out like a fat guy in a marathon in my match with John happens when I'm just 1-up going into fourteen, a very reachable par 5 for both of us, but with a strategically placed pond guarding the green like it's Buckingham Palace. Well done on the architect, Bob Cupp. I've got 6-iron in—it's a very exacting shot, and I don't pull it off. I open the blade up like a lunch box and block it way to the right, but luckily away from the pond. It lands on terra firma—I think.

I'm still alive.

Almost all the hazards at Pumpkin Ridge are these environmentally sensitive areas, so if your ball goes in there, *you* can't go in there. Bye-bye biscuit.

This doesn't bode well.

I'm walking over the hill toward the green, not thinking the worst but not thinking the best, either. As I crest the hill, I see my ball is a couple yards outside the hazard. Whew.

Thank you, golf gods.

There's a tree, kinda like a smallish tree, maybe fifteen feet in height, some sort of oak, but it is smack dab in my way. About five feet up from the base, the tree splits into a Y, like a wishbone on a Thanksgiving turkey. I'm twenty yards from the hole, give or take. I see the gap in the tree like you might see a shining ray of hope, sliver though it may be.

Three feet wide? Four?

The hole is up and over a pretty decent hill, and I can only see the top half of the flag. The only way to hit a good shot in is to hit it through this field goal of a tree not ten feet in front of me. I have no choice but to go for it.

You can lay up when you're dead, right?

I hit the shot perfectly, and I can tell it's going to be on the green. As much if not more than I could hope for. I run up like Sergio in the PGA so I can see the end result, and as I reach the green, I can see the ball tracking for the hole like it has eyes. The vision not 20–20, but 20–10, seeing so much more than I do.

It goes in.

Hits the stick like an arrow hits the bull's-eye and goes in and I make eagle, with John putting for a pretty makeable birdie! I am sure John is in as big of a disbelief as I am. John was licking his chops, and I hole it out from the absolute spinach. I imagine it rocked him like a hurricane, to borrow a great lyric from the Scorpions. It certainly would have rocked me, had the shoe been on the other foot and I was asked to put on the other one. I'd be like, no thanks—I'm no longer wearing shoes of any kind.

I'm walking barefoot, baby.

Truth be told, it was lucky as all get out. But I would rather be lucky than good.

I WIN THE 14TH HOLE TO GO 2 up, then win the 16th to take the match, 3–2. Are the stars aligning?

I don't know, but they sure are shining bright.

10

THE MORNING EVOLVES

32 BECOMES 16

IN THE SWEET SIXTEEN I PLAY KELLY MILLER, who is now the president of Mid Pines and Pine Needles—married to Peggy Kirk Bell's daughter. Kelly is another Mid Amateur at the time, who was an All American at the University of Alabama. Kelly is also very even-keeled—and, like John, a really good guy. Due to Kelly's experience, I know he has more smarts than me going in a match like this, and that's what he'll try to beat me with today.

His mind game.

Me?

I'll have to beat Kelly with my clubs, wear him down, make sure he knows I'm not going anywhere, even though I'm just a punk college kid.

Which is exactly what I do.

I'll win, 3–2, and again don't have to play the 17th. In the round of 32, the second and third rounds are played on the same day (should fate shine on you and you win your morning match), so it's potentially a 36-hole, or two-match, day. Maybe it's a benefit for me to be playing a Mid Amateur in my second match. Kelly's older, mid-40s, I am guessing. Maybe he's a touch tired. Legs a little wobbly, shoulders a little slumped.

I don't remember a lot about this match, oddly enough. After all, thirty-six holes in one day is a boatload of golf. They used to play thirty-six in most of the majors back in the day, in the era of nickel loaves of bread and newsstands—but not now. Not in the era of worldwide television and power bars.

I do, however, remember this.

Quick back story.

The 10th hole at the Witch Hollow course at Pumpkin Ridge, where we play the match-play portion of the US Am, is a crazy hole. Ghost Creek at Pumpkin Ridge is where we played the stroke-play portion. How you get in, and how you get out, hopefully with trophy in hand. One is public, one is private.

I'll let you guess which one.

The 10th hole at Witch Hollow is where I start stroke play on the first day. Where I hit that crazy flop shot in. The 10th is also where I hole a massive 50-foot putt against Kelly in our match to win the hole and some serious momentum. My line is all in the shadows, but I can see it like I can see the fingernails on my hands.

And again, like the eagle I holed out against John Harris, the ball runs into the cup like Jessie Owens to the Olympic 400 finish line, like it has eyes not just in the front, but also in the back. Not sure if I've ever made a putt like that before or since. It was like something out of *The Chronicles of Narnia*.

I ultimately win the match over Kelly, more than twenty years my senior, 3–2.

11
REMATCH: BUDDY MARUCCI RETURNS
16 BECOMES 8

THIS IS A MASSIVE MATCH FOR ME.

It's a rematch, actually, of the '95 US Amateur at Newport, where Buddy Marucci beat me on the 19th hole in the semis, postponing my date with destiny by three hundred sixty-five days, give or take a full moon.

It's no secret on the amateur circuit that Buddy is one hell of a putter. It's as if the flatstick were an extension of who he is— you could even call it an appendage, the way Buddy becomes so one with the blade. I have a little advantage over him with my distance—I clip him off the box pretty much all day long. But Buddy is putting as well if not slightly better than me—and I am putting lights out—all match long.

It's hard to name a putt of mine Buddy doesn't answer.

Our match is closer than cheese on a backyard burger all day long, until we get to 16 with the pin front right—as we know, not my favorite position for my soft, spinning draw. Buddy knocks it pretty close, a little short and left of the hole, and calmly buries his 12-footer for birdie to go 1-up with two to play. A make that doesn't surprise me, similar to what I did to him a year ago at Newport.

So I head to 17, 1-down and running out of real estate. Just the opposite of our semifinal match the year before, where I was 1-up with two to play, before flat-out gifting Buddy the 17th hole, going to extra holes, then going home.

The pin on 17 is also front right, one of the few right-hand positions I've encountered all week. Lucky for me and my draw, the hole plays fairly short if you can hit a good drive, which I do, and I find myself with 9-iron in hand, and I lace it right over the flag, to about 15 feet. It's a good shot—a smart shot.

There are certain times in match play where you gotta *make* things happen. You can't just sit there and *hope* something happens. You've got to go out there and visualize it, see it in your mind's eye, and will it to happen.

This 15-footer is one of those times.

Standing over the putt, I just knew I was gonna bury it. And I did, like Lucius Clay in his backyard in the old *Legend of Wooley Swamp* Charlie Daniels song.

And like his ghost, I got up and I walked around.

Buddy and I are standing on the par 5 18th, all square. This is déjà vu all over again. One year removed. I'm thinking this match could just as easily go into extra holes as it could end right here.

I have the honors, and I stripe my tee shot—my best of the day. Buddy blocks his shot a little right, into the rough, which is easily ankle deep, and draws the absolute worst lie ever. Buddy has no choice but to lay up.

And this is the weirdest thing.

I guess Buddy is hitting either an 8- or a 9-iron, and he takes a mighty rip at the ball, but it just chunks out of the rough, like he was swinging a shovel. Imagine a squirrel flitting from branch to branch but suddenly a bowling ball is tied to his back right butt cheek and he drops like a boat anchor.

After Buddy takes his swing, he looks up and over to the right, like something or somebody has disturbed him.

The ball travels maybe twenty yards?

So now Buddy's got an easy 240 maybe 250 to the green for his third shot. And by easy, I mean the amount of yardage, not the shot. No guarantee for a par by any means. I'm in position to go for the green in two, and I do, knocking it pin-high into a low collection area just right of the green into the first cut of rough. Still, from this angle, I could mishit this chip and have it roll back to my feet. You've gotta play safe out of here. No chance to be aggressive. But that's okay. I'm lying two, just like Buddy—and he is 250 yards behind me.

There are these evergreen trees that frame the left and right side of the green—they must be a hundred feet tall if they are an inch. Again, like kicking a field goal, which is what Buddy is up against. Buddy blocks his shot—with a 5-wood, I think, and it rattles the evergreens but miraculously pops back out into the fairway. Still very much alive. Lying three but not on the green yet, and I'm lying two, pin high. I'm feeling pretty good—not gonna lie.

Buddy knocks his 4th shot onto the green. Not a great shot, but he's twenty feet away. Certainly, makeable for Buddy. But—will he make it with everything on the line?

That's the question I ask myself. I'm looking at my shot like you might look at a flat tire on the highway and AAA on the way. I've got a couple of options. I could play toward the hole and risk the ball coming back down the hill to the toes of my Tungsten-spiked FootJoys. My ball is sitting in the first cut of rough, not the tightly mowed fairway. That helps, but I still can't risk going at the hole and the ball coming back to my feet. So, I choose to aim left and roll the dice that Buddy isn't going to make his putt and par wins the hole, the match, and forward I go.

So that is the shot I hit.

And it finishes just inside the distance of Buddy—so he has to go first. Buddy's putt will decide the match.

Buddy misses. I lag it down for the win. Lag is a great word.

A three-letter visual.

Thank you, Ray.

12

OFF TO THE SEMIS

8 BECOMES 4

In match play, you have to know when to play the opponent and when to play the course. You're constantly evaluating the odds. It's like you're at the blackjack table, and you're watching all the cards come out, you're seeing what's going on. How many face cards are out there? How many regular cards? You're constantly evaluating. Do I double down? Do I fold? What do I do?

You're basing every decision on the odds, and at that time and point with Buddy Marucci facing a tricky twenty-foot putt with a couple feet of break and even as good as he is—how often is he going to make that putt with the match on the line and the chance to extend? I am thinking one in fifty.

So I rolled the well-thought-out dice, and they rolled in my favor.

I like to say, whenever I see Buddy, whenever our paths cross: "I helped you get to the Masters, and you helped me get to the Masters."

He always laughs, and so do I. And it's genuine, and good.

It is crazy rare to play the same opponent two years in a row that deep into match play in the U.S. Amateur. You talk about statistical probabilities. It's almost impossible. Maybe just a little more improbable than making it to the finals of the US Amateur.

Both of us in the semifinals two years in a row?

Take the odds and think one step further. I'm playing against my teammate Robert Floyd (Ray Floyd's son) in my next match. And Tiger is playing against *his* teammate, Joel Kribel. So it's Florida vs Florida and Stanford vs Stanford. West Coast, East Coast.

That is not lost on me. The juxtaposition, I mean.

The odds of this happening have got to be astronomical.

Don't get me wrong. This is really cool. But both semifinal matches playing against your own teammate, your friend? What in the heck? Great exposure for Stanford University— great exposure for the University of Florida, for sure. But at the same point, to play against your teammate in a match of that magnitude. The winner goes on to the finals with an invitation to play in the Masters, and the loser goes home, to cold cereal and dorm room living.

It is a damn difficult situation to be in. For all four of us.

I know how much Robert would absolutely love to play in the Masters with his father, who won the Masters in '76, breaking the tournament scoring record in the process. To play with his father in the Monday-Wednesday practice rounds, the Par Three Tournament, maybe even in the tournament itself.

Man, that's a dream come true on crazy levels.

One of us is gonna have to look at the other and say, either out loud or on the inside, I got the best of you today.

The craziest thing, and this is how the '95 semifinals plays into all of this, is that the '95 semifinals totally set me up for this moment right here, right now.

Why was I paired with Tiger in a collegiate event eight months before this US Am? Why was I in that semifinal with Buddy the year before?

Everything happens for a reason, and it's like the script has been written before it even happens. Maybe I'm being too biblical, and I'm certainly not the most religious guy, but it's as if this were meant to happen. Especially what happens at the end.

Some things are just meant to be, meant to happen. There is no way to avoid it.

It's just destiny. And you gotta play your part.

13

8 BECOMES 4 PART TWO

ME VS ROBERT FLOYD

I KNOW ROBERT IS GOING TO BE a damn tough opponent.

Robert has two years at Florida under his belt—I am just getting started good with my second. Robert's had pretty good success and I've had okay success—no great shakes, but I'm a factor of sorts. That said, I have a really, *really* good feeling about the way things are going. I feel very in control of my game, and the situation, and all that goes with it.

Some background, which highlights another crazy coincidence. At the Dixie Amateur in south Florida in December of '95, I play against Robert in match play, and he beats me on the 20th hole. He makes an 8-footer for birdie. Tricky putt, but he rolls it in beautifully.

What sticks out most to me about our match at the '96 US Am match is something that kinda irks me, and I use it as fuel (like the great line from Mickey Rourke in *Barfly*). On the seventh hole at Pumpkin Ridge, Robert and I both have makeable birdie putts. It's a mighty close match—we are even. And Robert's ball is just outside of me.

Robert misses his putt.

Robert has a bit of a temper.

I give Robert the slap away with his putter and in doing so takes a chunk out of the green right in my line. A bread slap worth of green chunk. I could have made a sandwich with it, extra tomato. Robert repairs it and is sorry for it. Apology is accepted.

It's all good, Robert.

Still.

I miss my putt. Not saying that's why I missed my putt—it's not—I just straight up missed it—but it did throw me off, Robert's putter-slap of the green like that.

That moment sticks with me like bubble gum on the bottom of your jogging shoe.

Robert and I are tied going into the 14th hole, a very reachable par 5, and I win the hole to go 1-up in the match. I can't remember how I won the hole, funny enough. That part is a bit of a blur.

We get to the 15th, the very clever par 3 at Pumpkin Ridge, and I hit a really good tee shot in—a 6-iron that I feather in with a soft draw that actually works out. Fifteen feet behind the hole. Robert plays the hole well and makes par.

I've got this putt; it's kinda one of those that you have to summon the will to make a putt like this. It's a pretty straight putt, a little downhill but slicker than melted ice cream on the back of your waffle cone.

I hit a pure putt, and it disappears—it could have gone in on a thimble.

I know you've had one of those, in your life, once or twice.

I give it a fist pump (nothing like I will see Tiger do tomorrow, but at this point I don't know that's coming), but a pretty darn good fist pump, nonetheless. It's more of a fist clench that goes down to the ground than a pump. I am 2-up with 3 to play. And I'm thinking: I win the next hole, I win the match. Finals of the US Am here I come.

I get up on the next tee box, and I'm confident yet nervous as all get out.

If I win this next hole I'm playing in the Masters.

The Masters!

I have no idea how Tiger's match is going, nor do I care. I am paying no attention to that at all. I'm staring straight down the barrel of the gun that is pointed at me, and his name is Robert Floyd. That is where my focus is.

I get up there with my Burner Bubble TaylorMade Driver (how's *that* for old school?), and this is something you can't do nowadays even if you wanted to, the way the technology has changed so drastically and you a 30 handicap, beelining your mishits all day long.

I hit a pop-fly hook.

High off the toe of the club—like the worst-looking drive you have ever seen in your life. It goes up into the wind and to the left and into some bushy trees. Limbs from the bottom to the top.

Aww, man.

I have to take an unplayable lie. Two, hitting three.

Robert hits his tee shot down the middle—absolutely stripes it. I'm thinking, *Okay, here we go. I'm gonna give Robert this hole like a gift at Christmas and be just one up with two to play.*

I look at my options—there aren't many, any—I've got to take an unplayable lie. No other way around it.

I could've—probably should've—gone back to the tee. You have three options when you blow it off the tee and into the absolute spinach. With an unplayable lie, going back to the tee—well, that is the first option. You can also go no closer to the hole and drop down two club lengths. Or, you can opt to go from you and the flag, keeping the flag between you and your ball, and walk back to the end of the Earth if you want.

I don't really think about going back to the tee—and the other option was not really an option. So, I take my two club lengths option. But I gotta chip out sideways. Which was kind of dumb on my part.

I could have advanced the ball farther had I gone back and hit another tee shot. But your brain doesn't always work like you want it to—especially when you look back and reflect on said brain.

Now, I've got 190 to the hole. A fairly long way. Robert is maybe 165–170.

So, get this: I hit my fourth shot into the green before Robert has even hit his second. And I end up winning the hole. How crazy is that?

I hit a 4-iron in, and it's a pretty good shot, all things considered, the pin back left, and me drawing it in softly—at least I am trying to, but it just bounces off the back of the green and into the first cut of rough, maybe 25 feet from the hole.

Now I'm lying 4.

Four.

The best I can make if I chip it in is 5. All Robert has to do is hit in on the fat side of the green, two-putt, and he wins the hole. This hole is like cake, for Robert, with extra icing and a little ice cream on the side with all his favorite sprinkles.

Robert has a 7-iron in and surprisingly double-crosses

himself and hits it long left of the green—the absolute worst place in the world on this hole.

Trust me, I've been there, in Robert's shoes, in an earlier round.

Robert suddenly has no shot, and suddenly I'm thinking I'm still in this in, in spite of all my mess.

I'm back in the game.

Robert's in the trees but hardly 40 or 50 feet from the hole. He can kind of see the ball, but there is a bunch of leaves and overhanging branches and sticks and junk. Still, he thinks he can play the shot from this lie. I admire him for that. I would have thought that, too, had I not been in there the time before and realized there is no way in hell.

Robert settles into the shot and totally whiffs it. Nothing but air and no ball.

I can't help but think, *Well, this is interesting.*

Robert gets up there with his 4th shot.

That shot, Robert hits it maybe a foot from his feet? Fifth shot over the green. Then he chips it up tight for a gimme triple bogey 7. He's outside of me now.

Total reversal of fortune.

Robert chips it up with a putt for a triple bogey 7. A seven, after standing in the middle of the fairway with the same number club in his hand.

Man, I have been there before.

Golf is one hell of a game.

All I have to do is get up and down for a 6, yes, a 6, a double bogey, to win the hole and, yes, the match.

The *match.*

I hole the chip.

I flopped it onto the green and let gravity take care of the rest. I would rather be lucky than good. What about you? Best bogey I've ever made in my life. I win the match and, well, Tiger awaits. And so does the Masters.

The Masters! Holy moly. I am going to play in the Masters next year! My eyes are blown out of the back of my mind.

I GET INTERVIEWED BY NBC AFTER MY match with Robert, but I don't recall a word of it. I am on such a crazy high. But I do recall right as rain the USGA taking a picture of me and Kristi riding in a golf cart with a US Am official behind the wheel and the look on Kristi's face so, so proud of me and me so proud of her.

Memories for the nursing home.

Me, Steve Scott, playing in the finals of the 1996 US Amateur. Against Tiger Woods, the best there is. Or is he?

Bring it on, baby.

Holy moly, I cannot wait.

14

POSTGAME INTERVIEW

LOOK AT YOUR LEFT HAND, NOT YOUR RIGHT HAND

AFTER MY MATCH WITH ROBERT AND MY brief interview with NBC, security escorts me into the press room where I answer a handful of questions—again, I recall very little of what was asked and what was said.

But this, this I will never forget.

After my Andy Warhol fifteen minutes of fame in the press room, I'm taken to the tower overlooking the 18th green. Cameras are set up and rolling. Because there are only two people playing tomorrow, Tiger and myself, the announcers need soundbites and apparently, I am the man for the job.

Apparently, I am also a sucker.

They trick me up there in that tower overlooking the 18th green, just like something out of the movie *Glengarry Glen Ross*. They make me sound like such an aloof, cocky little wannabe.

They ask me, point blank, with me standing up there all

appreciative and just honored to be there: "Steve, where do you see yourself going from here? How much confidence is this going to give you if you win?"

I reply, "I'd love to get on Tour. I'd love to win events, love to win majors."

I smile.

They tell me, "Answer that question again, Steve, but answer it the same."

So, I do. Then they tell me to do it one more time. So, I do, even though I am a touch confused.

You can test this on yourself, but once you answer the same question three times in a row, the tone of your answer comes across very differently, and mine came across as very cocky and matter of fact. The third time I say it, it comes out, "I'd love to win on Tour, preferably Majors."

The first time I answer the question I come across as, well, I'd *like* to do that. The third time I come across as I'm absolutely *gonna* do that. It is so matter-of-fact. A done deal.

The press got what they wanted, I guess, but it's a pretty crappy way to go about it.

15

MEDITATION

I PREPARE MY MIND FOR EACH MATCH the same way, every time. I'm sitting in the back of the locker room at Pumpkin Ridge, a card-playing room, I'm guessing, overlooking a simple patio, and I am by myself, like I have been for every single match at Pumpkin Ridge. My hands are folded. No cards to show. I close my eyes and picture myself playing well, picture myself hitting the shots I want to hit, carrying myself a certain way—walking down the fairway a certain way. Organizing my thoughts for the day. Visualizing what I want to do, that I'm going to be confident in my ability no matter what the situation. Getting in a mindset where nothing is going to break my concentration, my belief in myself. No matter what. If I must hole a 30-foot putt to win the hole, then I will *will* myself to do it. I'm putting so well right now that I'm honestly surprised when I miss one, crazy as that sounds. I bet you've been on a roll like that in your golfing life once or twice.

The power of that sort of belief in yourself is really strong, and a part of the game that gets lost on a lot of people. Nobody really taught me how to do it—I just do it. It's as if I'm in a trance. And in that trance, with seven tees and 26 cents in my right-hand pocket, I just know I'm going to crush you. Regarding the quarter and penny, I'll tell you about that later. The seven tees? Well, seven is a lucky number.

I imagine myself as a football player, Division I, running out of the tunnel like my hair is on fire and my ass is catching, the crowd going wild.

You don't really get that sort of adrenaline rush in golf, so I create it within myself.

Might sound a little crazy, I know. In fact, I'm sure it does. But that is how I prepared for every match.

16

THE 1996 US AMATEUR

SUNSET

I AM TIRED AS ALL GET OUT.

It's the night before my—our, I should say: Kristi is with me side by side, step by step—finals match against Tiger, just a few hours removed from one hell of a grueling, two-match day. But we won each one of them, didn't we, honey?

I'm running on adrenaline and walking on sunshine, just like the song.

The US Amateur is a full week of competition, and that's not mentioning the practice rounds. You make it all the way to the 7th day of the US Amateur, the finals, and it's, well, your 7th day in a row of intense competitive golf, as big as it gets. One hundred fifty holes, maybe? Add in the practice rounds, and you're nearing the 200s. That is a lot, and I mean a *lot* of golf in one week. More than I have ever played in my life.

By comparison, a PGA Tour event is a couple of fun

practice rounds and then four days of seriousness: 72 holes, providing you make the cut. The US Am is pretty much doubling that.

The night before our match with Tiger, I knew I was playing at Augusta, as did Tiger. I am insanely jacked up for that. We are in, Kristi, in, no matter what tomorrow brings. Oh, wow. The Crow's Nest awaits.

How mind-blowing is that?

I feel so good about my game right now that I wish we could jump right back on the box and play this finals match in the dark. I could go right now and wade out into the darkness.

My confidence could not be any higher.

It's time to get deeper.

CAN I GO BACK TO THE SEMIFINALS at Newport for a brief second? It's funny, the perception of time when you are in those pressure situations. I am so nervous, yet so alive and electric. Everything in my brain is going by so quickly. Like the day just came and passed and it was done. The decision making is so quick.

Like *The Matrix*. And I'm Keanu Reeves, if you replace the black hair with blond.

LEADING INTO THAT FINALS MATCH WITH TIGER, after dinner at The Old Spaghetti Factory (man, was it good, but it was hard to eat much or pretty much anything at all because I was so nervous), I can't help but sit on the edge of my Courtyard Marriott hotel bed and reflect, the pillows still untouched and the bed still made. It is there on that edge that I remember all the assistance that came along the way in my golf life.

Ray Daley, never charging me for lessons, despite giving

me the best golf and life lessons I ever had. My aunt and uncle, my dad's sister and her husband—they make it possible for Kristi to be on my bag at Pumpkin Ridge. They pay for her flight, hotel room, a little traveling cash.

Without their generosity, I am out here on my own, alone.

My uncle has passed away these days, unfortunately. Eleven years or more he's been gone. Bill Johnson was his name. He was a great man. So incredibly generous with his extended family was my Uncle Bill. He'd give you the shirt off his back without so much as blinking. Shoes and socks, too.

My funniest Uncle Bill moment is forever frozen in time by a photograph, taken when Tiger makes that unbelievable putt for eagle on the 35th hole of our match and he's making his famous uppercut fist pump to the sky. Everybody is cheering like crazy, but Uncle Bill is looking away, angry as hell, spitting nails, hammers, and saws.

Thanks, Uncle Bill, and Aunt Charlotte, for always having my back.

I AM READY TO DO THIS.

It's around 11 p.m., and Kristi and I are figuring out a game plan for tomorrow. My coach, Buddy Alexander, called earlier to offer his support, and I appreciate that greatly. Buddy tells me to be patient—play Steve Scott golf—don't get caught up in what Tiger's doing. Buddy won the 1986 US Am, so he knows the spot I am in.

He lived it.

I know tomorrow is a big day for Tiger; he's gunning for history, immortality. It's a big day for the game of golf—the history of the game, and I am standing in the way of making it happen. I get that and respect that. But my goal is still to crush Tiger, just like he wants to crush me.

A little side note, if I may, before the match begins.

About eight months before tomorrow explodes, in early November of '95, I'm paired with Tiger in a collegiate tournament at Palmetto Dunes near the coast of Carolina. One of the strongest fields we will play in all year—top teams all.

Final round.

Tiger and I are in the last group off the tee. As a collegian golfer, there is nothing better than being in the final group of the day.

I have never played with Tiger before. Don't know a thing about him, except that I hear he's good. Like crazy good. Bobby Jones good. Jack Nicklaus good.

Holy moly is he ever.

From Tiger's first swing, I'm so caught up in his game. How insanely far he hits it. He's hitting these towering 3-irons—who hits a *towering* three-iron? 240 yards on the fly, if it's an inch. Arcing like a bell curve. High as a sand wedge. No chance I can hit that shot, nor could anyone, at the time. Maybe not even now. Tiger's drives are 60 to 70 yards past me and the other guys in our group; some of the guys he's damn near a hundred yards past, and we are pretty good players on our respective teams, Division I players all. Heck, we are in the last group of the day on the last day of the tournament.

We are as good as it gets.

Tiger takes lines off the tee that none of us would ever even dream of doing, including the architect who designed the place. Silly, what Tiger can do. Who flies a driver 300 yards in 1995, with the same standard golf ball and clubs I am playing with?

Three hundred yards in the air?

I shoot 80 that day—totally blow it, and also because I'm blown away by this guy—and Tiger shoots 70 even though he misses a million putts. He makes it look so easy. Shoots 70 without really making any putts whatsoever. Wins medalist honors—deservedly so, certainly. But that day of an old-fashioned head-to-head ass whippin' prepared me greatly for this finals match at Pumpkin Ridge.

Kristi knows, and I know. I couldn't get caught up in anything Tiger was doing. I didn't want to watch Tiger swing, even though it was insanely impressive and expressive, like a Van Gogh painting meets Monet. As if there were going to be a collision. Obviously, I heard the sound of his golf ball coming off the club. A different sound than anybody swinging a golf club has ever made, at least one that's made its way into my ears. Very much like a gunshot.

Just God-given talent. No other way to explain it.

But.

I remember walking down the dew-swept area to the first hole that next morning for our 7:15 a.m. tee time, with my metal spikes clicking on the pavement, clickety-clack. We arrive at the course at 6:00 a.m. as the sun trades places with the moon, just in time for a quick, light breakfast (hard to eat, in a pressure cooker like this), then it's off to the practice tee—loosen up the old bones, even when they are just 19 years old—and let's go.

Early, I know, but not as early as our 4:30 wake-up call from the hotel operator.

I felt like my head had just hit the pillow.

It's funny, I'm so into my own world, so into what I'm doing under my Pernicci surfer ball cap that I'd worn all week, that I have absolutely no memory of seeing Tiger until we meet up on the first tee. I don't even notice him warming up just beside me.

Later I will learn he was warming up and hitting balls not 20 yards away.

It's a little—make that a lot—hard for me to believe that the first hole at Pumpkin Ridge is literally lined with people, fans as far as the eye can see, even at this crazy early hour. It's right at 420 yards long, the first hole, a solid par 4 in those times.

Look at all these people. You kind of know it's going to be a different day.

Oddly enough, Tiger doesn't have his sports psychologist, Jay Brunza, on his bag, who had been on Tiger's bag in all of his previous five consecutive USGA victories. But today, it's his ol' high school buddy, a guy named Bryon Bell (who is now, in 2021, the president of his design team, interestingly enough).

I'm stunned.

Bryon is walking ten or fifteen yards ahead of me, Tiger's bag on his shoulder, and I turn to Kristi and say: "Tiger doesn't have his sports psychologist caddying for him this time. What the heck? We are gonna crush him. He doesn't have his security blanket with him."

I firmly know I'm going to take it to him. Everything is on the line today. There is no tomorrow. You have got to leave it all on the course.

And I did.

Turns out, I got left out there, too.

17

CAMELOT

ONE BRIEF SHINING MOMENT

YOU'RE 5-UP IN THE MORNING ROUND, Steven Marshall Scott. You have absolutely destroyed the best amateur golfer in the world. And you are going to shoot two-under par 70 in the afternoon. Well done, my friend. Well done. And, yet, you are going to lose.

You are going to lose.

That just doesn't happen, except, well, every once in a lifetime it does. Sorry about that.

The only guy who could do it to you is, well, the guy who does it.

Your game was *so* good that week, Steve. You were on fire. Well, maybe not the 79 you shot on the first day of stroke play . . . *Towering Inferno* it was not. But the 66 that followed to make match play by a stroke. Well done there, my friend. In the finals match you shoot, if it were stroke play and not match play, 68–70.

That is pretty damn strong.

And the moving back of the mark that you told Tiger to do. Wow. Who does that?

You will be told more than once that the only guy on the planet in that position who would have told Tiger to move his mark back is you. You hope not. You hope that everyone who plays the great game of golf in all the right ways, for all the right reasons, would have done the exact same thing.

After all, it's the right thing to do.

But I'm guessing you know that.

18

TRIAL BY FIRE

THE FINALS MORNING ROUND BEGINS

Before I hit my first tee shot, it's as if electricity were running through my body—like jolts and bursts and, well, all kinds of stuff. I can feel the volts, even in my ears. Like I'm plugged into a socket in an arena. I can feel it from the crowd, the thousands of people who have shown up to watch history in the making, whether it's from Tiger or from me—like you could put it on a plate, and me with a knife, fork, and spoon to eat it all up.

Or throw it all up.

Projectile vomit. Pardon the crudity, but I feel like everything inside my skin is about to come out and spill onto the first tee box.

I've never felt this way before, still I just know I'm going to stripe my first drive.

I am nervous as all get out, but I know it will have no negative effect on any shot I hit today. If anything, I know my nervousness will make my focus better, my shots tighter, my ball flight more visionary. How I know this, I have no idea. But it is as clear to me as Gulf Coast waters.

If you are not nervous, you are not alive.

So, I talk to myself before the match begins: *Today will be the coolest way to play golf, because, well, Steve, you know you're gonna hit a great shot. Every time. Adrenaline is a drug—no question about it. It gives your mind a state of superpower.*

Had I known I would never feel this way again on a golf course, well . . . I don't know what I would have done. Would I have treated the moment differently? I just don't know. Trust me—it's danced the *Last Waltz* in my head once or twice over the past 25 years. Engelbert Humperdinck, can we talk? After today I mean—or maybe in-between 18s.

Today I will climb Mt. Everest. Get to the top, and as I go to stick my American flag into the frozen ground, it will be snatched out of my hand like an unwrapped lollypop on a schoolyard playground. And I will never climb Mt. Everest again. As for Tiger, he will keep climbing like a spider into his web, waiting on the next fly. And tomorrow, Tiger will turn pro and in the week that follows take a crack at climbing to the top of Kilimanjaro on his first try. Whereas I will play in a Division I golf tournament at Shoal Creek in Birmingham, Alabama.

In a way, it'll be deeply disappointing—not Shoal Creek's fault; it's a really great golf course, phenomenal, actually—because this moment in time will never be replicated again. In either of our lives. Such a defining moment. I'd freeze it if I could, but I can't.

No matter how long the winter, spring always comes.

I CAN FEEL MY HEART JUMPING OUT of my chest. No need to put my hand over it. I can see the rapid rise and fall of my blue-striped Tommy Hilfiger shirt as my heart dances the polka and I swear it's wearing Oktoberfest clogs at the Hofbräuhaus. Thank God Tiger has the honor. Of the seven tees I have in my right front pocket, I'm not sure I could tee up my Titleist 7 on any one of them.

The match begins in a blur, though we both hit the fairway and end up tying the first two holes. And suddenly I feel like I can breathe, and I take the third and it feels like Christmas, and I am a bit taken aback. Tiger hits it in the water, to gift me the hole. On the 4th hole, I make a curling twelve-footer to win and go up by two. On the 5th, a par three guarded by water, Tiger splashes it twice, and I stay dry to go up by three.

This is all happening so fast.

Too darn fast. Something isn't right.

We tie seven, eight, and nine.

On ten, the wicked par three, I hit a great 4-iron to six feet and drain the putt to go 4-up. The next hole, a par five, I drop an 8-footer for birdie to go 5-up.

I am 5-up through eleven holes. I am crushing him. Tiger's hitting it into the trees, the water, the rough, you name it.

This doesn't make any sense.

At Pumpkin Ridge, the par 5s are numbers four, seven, eleven, fourteen, and eighteen. In this morning round of our finals match, I will ultimately win four of those five par 5s. Against an opponent who can hit 300-yard drives. And by 300-yard drives, I mean some of them end up 320, 330.

This doesn't make any sense.

Unlike a round with the fellas, there is no stopping at the halfway house for a hotdog and a cold beer—not that we would be popping cold ones in public at the ripe old age of 19. You

TRIAL BY FIRE • • 67

leave nine green in the finals match of the US Amateur, and you head straight to the box on ten.

Tiger and I meander our way through the heart of the back nine at Pumpkin Ridge, trading blows until I lose fourteen but win sixteen after hitting the greenside bunker and darn near holing my bunker shot. Tiger goes on to 3-putt to make it a moot point.

So now, I'm 5-up after sixteen holes.

On seventeen, Tiger sticks a 9-iron tighter than a tick on a hound dog for the win, but on eighteen I return the favor with a wedge from sixty yards out that sticks equal to the tick on the hound dog. We see-saw the last few holes, neither outweighing the other.

I win the first eighteen-hole match 5-up.

I didn't see this coming. Certainly not like this. I don't see what comes next, either. But I won't lie—I had a feeling.

I really did.

After our first 18-hole match, Tiger jumps into the phone booth and comes out as Superman.

If you are familiar with the lyrics of that classic REM song, you know that phone booth change doesn't bode well for me.

Tiger really can do anything.

19

THE 90-MINUTE WAIT

Intermission begins, as I am 5-up on one of the greatest amateurs to ever play the game, perhaps the *best* ever.

It's a hard argument between Tiger and Bobby Jones, although my heart falls to Jones. He stayed amateur to the end, at the tender age of 28.

Time for a quick bite to eat and back to the box we go. I'm so raring to go. I could have forgone the eats and walked straight from eighteen back to one.

Except, well, I can't. There is a 90-minute wait.

As the years roll by, I think to myself, well, maybe the powers that be didn't think the match between Tiger and this no-name Steve Scott kid was going to go as far as it did, and with television not airing until, what, three o'clock that afternoon, they needed a pause in the action.

In this case, one heck of a pause. An Australian speed bump for someone on a roll like mine.

Looking back, that 90-minute wait is probably the worst thing that could have happened to me. It put not a brick but a cinder block on my momentum, and it gave Tiger a long time to regroup, to work with his legendary sports psychologist, Jay Brunza.

That 90-minute wait gave Tiger a boatload of time to recoup his formidable game.

And even change clothes.

If there is another big-as-it-gets sporting event in this world where you get a 90-minute halftime, I don't know of it. I do know of the Super Bowl, where the halftime is forty-five minutes, as opposed to the usual fifteen—largely in part due to the halftime show and all those commercials. That's a lot of time to regroup, certainly a lot of time for the NFL, which usually just gives fifteen minutes, hardly enough time to get into the locker room, take a whiz, and get back out, which is why I think a lot of Super Bowls change on the proverbial dime after halftime.

Certainly, the Falcons/Patriots game did back in 2017.

20

INTERJECTION: KRISTI HOMMEL, STEVE'S CADDY, GIRLFRIEND, AND BRIDE-TO-BE, BUT SHE DOESN'T KNOW THAT

(THE BRIDE-TO-BE PART, I MEAN)

STEVE IS 5-UP. THAT IS A BUNCH.

And I'm on the bag.

Steve is also my boyfriend. And I think he is hot as hell. Okay to say that?

I'm walking off the 18th green, and Steve's bag is on my shoulder, like an old friend with his arm around me. I'm feeling really good, really excited. And in a way, a little puzzled about this Tiger Woods fellow. What's all the fuss all about this Tiger—that was an easy 18 holes.

Tiger doesn't make a lot of putts in the first match—almost

like he's just not a very good putter. I'm really happy for Steve, though—I believe this is definitely his match. He is going to win. How can he not now that he's 5-up?

As we're walking off the 18th green, Steve says to me, "Kristi, honey, I know I'm 5-up, but this is not a safe lead against this guy. You cannot even *begin* to think this is a safe lead against this guy."

This guy, Tiger Woods.

I'm taken aback, looking at Steve, like, *What?*

But Steve says it again.

This sounds nuts to me. We just crushed this Tiger Woods guy.

But I trust in Steve and think, *Well, then, we don't have to change anything. We've just got to keep playing hard and keep with the same strategy.* Yet, I am so, so excited. There is no denying that.

I can't wait to get to the clubhouse and call my parents, to make sure they are watching all of this on TV, but I can't get them on the phone. So I call my grandparents. And they drive over there to the house. Because they had been working outside in the yard, my parents couldn't hear the phone ringing. This was before cell phones were commonplace.

Funny, how those tiny devices changed the world.

So, that's what I remember. We ate lunch in the clubhouse with Steve's Uncle Bill and Aunt Charlotte. As we're eating, and there is quite a bit of time left to go before we tee off again, an hour and a half, which feels like an eternity at a moment like this, I say to Steve, "We need to go get some merchandise, some souvenirs.

We have got to remember this day."

Steve says, "Sure—let's go."

We stroll over to the merchandise tent, get matching golf shirts that say Pumpkin Ridge on them, with the logo, and I get a hat with the Pumpkin Ridge logo. The shirts are white, with green, vertical stripes, and made by Izod.

We still have them, 25 years later.

Steve looks really good in green. He looks good in anything. But I know that is neither here, nor there.

I get it.

AFTER THE SECOND ROUND OF STROKE PLAY, when we qualify, Steve kind of just enters this bubble of determination, amazing to watch—I would say a fierce determination, and boundless confidence. A determination and confidence I have seen many times when we play together for fun and even practice. Steve is on cruise control right now.

I just want to make sure he stays focused.

My job is, however and oddly enough, knowing when to distract him. Get his mind off the intensity, and then get him back, to the here and now. Steve knows these greens, knows his clubs, his targets. I read the greens, just in case he wants or needs validation, affirmation, or if he has a question, or wants reassurance. So, I look at the putts, just to kind of confirm with him.

Yes, yes, I agree with you.

As a player, I don't want someone reading my putts; I want to see it first. I know Steve does, too. But if I see something different, I'll ask, "What do you see? What makes you think the putt is going to do that, and not this? What do you see?" I kind of get in his head, in a good way.

Steve is the captain of the ship; I'm just trying to keep him on course. It wasn't that difficult to do, honestly. I'm kinda like the cheerleader, the sports psychologist. The sea seems pretty good to me, right now, after the first 18. Calm. No whitecaps.

I don't see the storm that Steve sees coming.

THE WHOLE FIRST ROUND, I KEEP EXPECTING, like, these spectacular shots, these amazing putts, from Tiger. But he misses very makeable putts—misses them just like crazy. And he just doesn't hit these great shots. I just don't see them. And I tell that to Steve. I don't get all the hype about Tiger.

And Steve says, "Honey, Tiger is known for making amazing comebacks. Tiger isn't Tiger yet. We've got 18 holes to go. This match is not even remotely over."

Steve knew; I didn't.

Although I quickly learn firsthand, as the second 18 unfolds.

When the "move your mark back" issue comes up, I don't notice it right away, because I'm raking the bunker, but I hear Steve's voice, and I can see Steve walking toward me and the bag, to the right side of the green. I figure it has something to do with moving the mark back.

And it was.

Still, it doesn't even dawn on me how monumental it was. I just thought, *Well, that's just what Steve does. The right thing. That makes sense, so—*

Not even understanding the gravity that would have meant, had Steve not done that.

It doesn't even dawn on me at the time.

I do remember joking with Steve during every match: "This is a long week; it's a lot of holes, so can you just please close out this match already, so we don't have to walk all these long holes?"

Q SCHOOL IS VERY SIMILAR TO THE US Amateur. Though I know they don't do Q school anymore. A shame, really. If you can make it through Q school, you are one heck of a player. You can make it through anywhere.

I've often been asked what I was wearing the day of the final match. I guess because I'm a woman and women are supposed to remember what they wear? How funny of a question, but I'll tell you.

Khaki Gap shorts, part of my school's golf team (Florida Southern) uniform, so I wear them a lot. The top is plaid and sleeveless, and I also have on my black Oakley cap, which I wore all the time. It fits my head perfectly, and I just love Oakley sunglasses.

The Eye-jackets.

Steve got them for my birthday that year.

STEVE AND I MEET FOR THE FIRST time in late November, my senior year of high school. I am seventeen and so is he, although I'll turn eighteen a month later. We meet at the Coral Square Mall. Our first date is on the 26th, which we count as an anniversary. Ever since that date, we have been together. Kinda funny.

I'm there, at the mall, with my best friend, Amy, who is on the golf team with me, and we go back to my car to get something, no memory as to what, and Steve pulls up in his Coca-Cola-red Mazda RX7.

I'm like, *Oh?*

Yes, I'm checking him out.

I don't realize Amy knows him until now. I had seen Steve previously at the same golf course, where both of our teams practice during the season.

My first encounter with Steve is kinda disappointing, I gotta say. But it makes me laugh, makes us both laugh, looking back on it.

The first time I ever *see* Steve up close and personal, it's in the parking lot of Coral Springs Country Club, and I'm walking to the putting green. Steve's putting on his shoes, and I'm kinda friendly, naturally, and he's cute, so I say hi. Steve has his sunglasses on and gives me a little head nod, like a *What's up?* kinda head nod, and I'm, like, *Eww—you can't even say hi?*

You're too cool to say hi to me?

So when Amy says hello to Steve all friendly like, I say, "You know him?"

And Amy says, "Yes—he's a great guy. Really nice. Sweet and kind."

And I'm thinking, *Okay, if you say so.*

About a week later, Steve ends up walking around the Coral Square Mall with us—because that's basically what high school kids do, at least back in my day. I'm just kinda tagging along, Amy and Steve just talking. At the time, I didn't realize he was such a good junior golfer. I'm not aware of his status in the state—he's the best, actually, although it doesn't come up in the conversation I'm not involved in. But Amy knew; she was also a really good junior golfer.

I had *no* idea as to Steve's ranking.

Nor did I care.

After Steve leaves, does whatever he has to do at the mall, buy some Polo cologne or something, Amy turns to me and says: "Want me to hook you up? I saw how you were eyeing him."

I blush, at least I think I blush, and I say, "Okay."

Amy decides it's a great idea, and well, we get some of our

friends and some of Steve's friends together and go bowling later that weekend. Pitchers of Cokes and soggy fries.

As the bowling goes on, I can see Steve is kind of shy, but really genuine. And funny. A dry, quick wit that makes me smile. Lots of one-liners that slide at you like a whiskey across a bar. Not that I've ever been to a bar at this point in my life. I'm only seventeen, after all.

As we get to the tenth frame, Steve and I are tied, and I'm next to bowl, and I think I can either throw a gutter ball and let him win or go for the win. And I think, *I'm just gonna kill him; I don't care.*

I end up throwing a gutter ball!

I guess Steve has the same dilemma on his mind, and he's the last one to bowl. He pauses, and then I see him purse his lips.

He was actually going to try to beat me—but *he* threw a gutter ball, too.

I don't remember what the score was. Couldn't have been much if we were slinging gutter balls at the end. But Steve always tells how I beat him that day with the best score, when he tells the story.

And, well, we've been together ever since.

A gutter ball marriage made good.

21

THE 18 HOLES OF YOUR LIFE THAT DEFINE YOU

THE SECOND 18 OF THE FINALS AT PUMPKIN RIDGE

It's QUITE THE DICHOTOMY, BEING OUT HERE with Tiger, and somehow being 5-up.

I do very little fine-tuning in the 90-minute intermission before the second eighteen. Why would I?

I'm 5-up, quite pleased with my swing, my ball striking, my flat stick. I'm playing well—*very* well, in fact. Why go out on the range with the chance to screw things up? By contrast, Tiger grinds away on the range with his swing, making use of every accoutrement he has at his fingertips.

And I'm about to go shopping with Kristi, my honey.

Butch also apparently feeds Tiger a bullshit story, one that I will hear the reason for some fifteen years later at a MET event in New York, an event where Butch doesn't know I'm in attendance. Butch allegedly tells Tiger, "Hey, you see that little girl [Kristi is actually 5–10; I wouldn't call that little] on Steve's bag? Every time you miss a putt, she laughs at you. Giggling like a schoolgirl *every time you miss*."

Nothing could be further from the truth. Butch likely said that to Tiger to pump him up, piss him off something fierce, and I get that, but that is a shitty, shitty way to do it. Especially when, years later, Butch claims the lie to be truth in front of God, *Golf Digest*, and everybody.

Including me.

Really?

AFTER A FEW BITES OF FRUIT AND a turkey sandwich with Kristi, in our own private little boardroom with the curtains drawn for privacy (very difficult to eat when you are this wound up, your stomach the size of an egg yolk, but I know I need to get some fuel in my belly for energy), and a quick tour of the pro shop, where we both buy souvenir shirts—I'll wear mine at Augusta during a practice round—Kristi and I head to the range to warm up, a little, before we tee off.

Fifteen minutes—maybe twenty. Hit a few irons, a few woods, couple drivers, roll a handful of putts.

I do know, however, that Tiger during the next 18 holes is going to do what he is famous for doing—bringing the heat like never before. In every single one of his championship wins, he's been down going into the final 18. Big time down. I know it's coming but to what level, I don't know. It's like being down (but in his mind by *no* means out) is his comfort zone. I know Tiger's coming for me. I can feel it just like I can feel the Portland, Oregon, sun on my skin. But I'm going to do everything I can to make it diamond hard for him to rally whichever troops he hopes to rally.

Me with my plastic club and ball on the back porch of our house in Coral Springs, Florida. My plastic club and ball, where this story begins. *(Courtesy of Steve Scott.)*

First day of nursery school. I'm standing in front of our home at 11957 Northwest 25th Court. I still remember the address, crazily enough. *(Courtesy of Steve Scott.)*

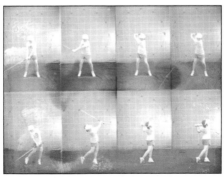

My swing as a nine-year-old. You can see that "lurch" with the left hip lunging toward the target that my teacher Ray always talked about. I always had a natural swinging motion, though . . . just something I was lucky enough to be born with. *(Courtesy of Steve Scott.)*

I get a golf bag as my trophy for winning that Broward County D Flight and win the other in a raffle. My first tournament win! This is our den on Northwest 25th Court, 1987. *(Courtesy of Steve Scott.)*

Some of my fondest growing-up memories. What a special place, Callaway Gardens—I knew it even then at the young age of ten. Summer of innocence, summer of '87. *(Courtesy of Steve Scott.)*

My brother, Roger, and me at Callaway Gardens, chasing that little white ball. I cherished moments like these with my older brother. *(Courtesy of Steve Scott.)*

Fast-forward to high school. This was pretty darn cool. A few weeks before graduation, Disney World closes to the public on Friday night, and we high school seniors get the run of the place from 10 p.m. to 6 a.m. I remember waiting on a park bench 45 minutes for Kristi to get there, because she was coming on another bus from another school. It was well worth the wait. *(Courtesy of Steve Scott.)*

Medalist Golf Club, Spring of '95—Norman's big charity event. My stepdad's boss was Greg Norman's next-door neighbor. Small world. Greg was so nice to us—to everybody. Just as genuine as can be. *(Courtesy of Steve Scott.)*

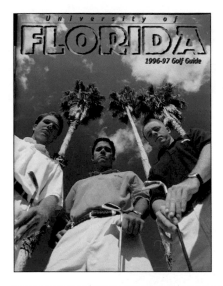

How funny—I'm staring you down with a Ping iron in hand. Now that's what I call intimidating. We thought we looked so tough. Ha! *(Courtesy of Steve Scott.)*

I knew Tiger was number one, and I knew I was number two. I truly believed I could change that—flip it like a switch. *(Courtesy of Golfweek Magazine.)*

When I strapped this tiny plastic circle on my bag the first day upon arrival, I thought, man, I have truly arrived. Is this really real? This little plastic bag tag told me yes. *(Courtesy of Steve Scott.)*

Access all areas if you had a book of these babies. On the day of the finals match, incredibly enough, 15,000 people did. *(Courtesy of Steve Scott.)*

HOLES	1	2	3	4	5	6	7	8	9	OUT	10	11	12	13	14	15	16	17	18	IN	TOTAL
Marker's Notes																					

Official Stroke Play Score Card
96th United States Amateur Championship®
Questions as to the Rules of Golf shall be referred to the USGA Rules Committee

PUMPKIN RIDGE GOLF CLUB
WITCH HOLLOW COURSE

For USGA Use
Previous Total _____
This Round _____
New Total _____
Verified: 18th _____ Pr. _____ Pub._____

Competitor _____
Round _____ Date _____

HOLES	1	2	3	4	5	6	7	8	9	OUT	10	11	12	13	14	15	16	17	18	IN	TOTAL
YARDS	401	168	414	533	205	446	619	382	463	3,631	194	553	143	410	470	175	432	422	545	3,344	6,975
PAR	4	3	4	5	3	4	5	4	4	36	3	5	3	4	5	3	4	4	5	36	72

Marker's Signature

Competitor's Signature

THE RULES OF THE UNITED STATES GOLF ASSOCIATION GOVERN PLAY
(Also see Local Rules and Conditions of the
Competition and the Notice to Players.)

OFFICIAL STROKE PLAY SCORE CARD

STROKE PLAY (see Rule 6-6)

● After each hole the marker should check the score with the competitor and record it. On completion of the round the marker shall sign the card and hand it to the competitor.

The competitor should check his score for each hole, and settle any doubtful points with the USGA Rules Committee. He shall ensure that the marker has signed the card, countersign the card himself and return it to the USGA Rules Committee immediately.

96TH UNITED STATES AMATEUR CHAMPIONSHIP®
Conducted by the United States Golf Association

Pumpkin Ridge Golf Club
Cornelius, Oregon
August 20-21, 1996
Witch Hollow Course

This is what I am up against. A hurdle, a broad jump, a moat. Maybe all three. *(Courtesy of Steve Scott.)*

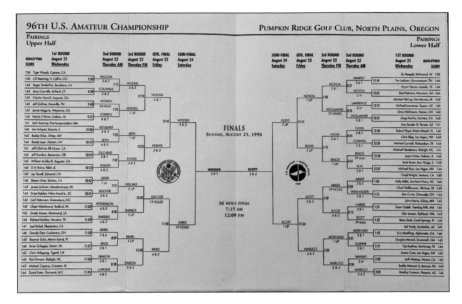

There are a lot of rows to hoe to make it to the finals match of the US Amateur. *(Courtesy of Steve Scott.)*

Kristi and I are headed to the finals! We were walking on air pillows and felt like we could beat anybody, Tiger Woods be damned—although I certainly had tremendous respect for him. I knew it was going to be the match of a lifetime, be it his or mine. Turns out it was both. *(Courtesy of Steve Scott.)*

Note how many pins are favorable to my sweeping, right-to-left draw. *(Courtesy of Steve Scott.)*

I guess this captures the moment of how I felt at the end of that epic finals match. I left it all out there, gave it everything I had—it just wasn't meant to be. How can you be sad about giving it all you got? *(Photo collage by Gary Hellwege.)*

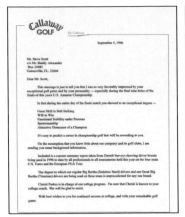

Beyond humbling, this one. But still mighty cool. *(Courtesy of Steve Scott.)*

This one put a lump in my throat—not gonna lie. *(Courtesy of Steve Scott.)*

Pretty cool letter from Scott Van Pelt, perhaps my favorite commentator, regardless of the sport. What beauty he brings to every word he says on ESPN. *(Courtesy of Steve Scott.)*

Kristi Hommel of Loxahatchee gets ready for a gag around at Ballenisles Country Club, following the U.S. Amateur when she caddied for her boyfriend, Steve Scott. He gave her the gopher head cover.

Caddy's attitude carries well over the tube, boosts golfer

By MICHELE GELORMINE
Palm Beach Post Staff Writer

LOXAHATCHEE — Kristi Hommel does more than carry the sticks.

When caddying for her boyfriend and top-ranked amateur Steve Scott, she's also a psychologist, a masseuse and a motivational coach.

Hommel, 19, is a golfer in her own right, with hopes of making the Ladies Professional Golf Association tour.

Tall and blond, she drew more television attention during the finals of the U.S. Amateur Championship last weekend than most caddies ever get. TV commentators zeroed in on her ability to boost Scott's confidence in pressure situations.

"We were thrilled that they mentioned her and that she was doing a good job," said Kaye Hommel, Kristi's mother. "Step-to-her front. We were hoping everything worked out well and that she would keep his spirits up and say the right thing."

Scott and Hommel stood alone, against the heavily favored Tiger Woods, who came armed with "Team Tiger," an entourage of coaches and supporters.

Scott surprised the crowd by leading most of the way. But Woods came from behind for an unprecedented third consecutive win. Woods later signed a five-year $40-million endorsement contract with Nike to turn pro.

"I was so proud of how Steve didn't fold and attacked right back under pressure," Hommel said.

'I was so proud of how Steve didn't fold and attacked right back under pressure.'

Caddy KRISTI HOMMEL

making sure that everybody is feeling good."

Hommel did not plan to attend the tournament. She caddied for Scott at the U.S. Open in June and spent most of her money on that trip. When Scott, aunt and uncle found out, they paid Hommel's expenses to Cornelius, Ore.

"They were at the Open and saw what a great job she did for me," Scott said.

Mutual friend and fellow golfer Amy Spoone introduced the couple nearly two years ago. Spoone arranged a group bowling outing that included Hommel and Scott. They've been together ever since.

"We are so much alike," Hommel said. "The relationship is so good and just gets better as the days go by. He's sweet, funny and caring."

And Scott said, "She's got a great personality and she's beautiful. She's there for me when I need her and that's the most important thing.

Hommel, a sophomore, attends Florida Southern College in Lakeland on a partial golf scholarship majoring in sports management. Career choices include working as a club pro or college coach, but her ultimate goal is to make the LPGA tour. She shoots in the mid 70s to low 80s.

Kristi got a lot of attention for toting my bag and doing all she did for me in the '96 US Am. This is a pretty cool snippet. *(Courtesy of The Palm Beach Post.)*

STEVE SCOTT: 'I NEVER GAVE UP'

The Gator golf team met Steve Scott, right, at Gainesville Regional Airport on Monday to welcome him home from the U.S. Amateur golf championship. From left are freshman Robert Harper, coach Buddy Alexander and Robert Floyd, a Amateur semifinalist.

Gator sophomore plays like a veteran

By PAUL JENKINS

There was a time, says Florida junior golfer Robert Floyd, when you could gauge the head of Steve Scott, play a round down and walk away a winner. It was like taking candy from a freshman.

Those days, apparently, are a thing of the past.

Scott, who started his sophomore year at Florida today, on Sunday showed the nation and one of the best amateur players in the world that he could be rattled by a couple of good shots.

Capping an outstanding summer, Scott tied Stanford sensation Tiger Woods through 37 holes before pinning up short on the second playoff hole in a U.S. Amateur final that still go down as one of the best amateur matches

of all time.

"The thing I've learned this summer is to just never give up," Scott said after arriving at Gainesville Regional Airport on Monday evening. "I never gave up believing in myself. I'm just more mature and smarter on the golf course. I've learned about pressure and what it does and how to handle it."

Early in his freshman season, Scott went head-to-head with Woods. It was like some CBS benchwarmer going up against Michael Jordan as Scott struggled to an 82.

But on Sunday, Woods was scrambling to catch up to Scott for most of the final, having to call on every last bit of his golfing prowess to claim his third consecutive U.S. Amateur title.

"I'm as proud as I can be with a junior at Stanford in the fall. Please see SCOTT, 2C

Woods poised to turn pro

By LARRY DORMAN
New York Times

MILWAUKEE — Now that high life really begins for Tiger Woods, the 20-year-old golfer who has decided to begin his professional career.

It will start with his signature on a contract with Nike worth $40 million over the next five years. His coming-out party is scheduled for Wednesday, when he is expected to announce he will play in the Greater Milwaukee Open.

Woods, who was to be a junior at Stanford in the fall, won his third consecutive U.S.

Amateur in stunning fashion Sunday.

In addition to the Nike deal, he will sign an agreement with Titleist for $3 million over three years, making this the largest golf deal ever.

Those who are familiar with his plans say Woods will play in seven tournaments before the end of the year.

Coach Buddy Alexander and some of my teammates welcome me home after the US Am. Note my shirt. That's the one Kristi bought for me during the break between 18s in the finals match. *(Courtesy of The Gainesville Sun.)*

COLLEGIATE

GOLFWEEK, October 18, 1997

Scott learns to deal with expectations

Steve Scott says he's hitting more consistent shots this year.

By RON BALICKI

Expectations were high — very high. Some came from outside, but mostly they came from within.

After finishing second to Tiger Woods at the 1996 U.S. Amateur, Steve Scott had a great deal of attention thrust his way, especially within the college and amateur ranks. When Woods turned professional after rallying to defeat Scott on the second extra hole for his third consecutive U.S. Amateur title, the eyes of non-professional golf fell on the Scott.

"It wasn't an easy year," said Scott, a junior at the University of Florida. "I tried not to think about what others expected of me, but at times it was difficult.

"Mostly, it was me putting pressure on myself. I can be hard on myself, too hard at times. I expected to play great every time I played, and when you do that the percentages (for playing great) are usually not in your favor. I ended up putting pressure on myself on every shot."

The result — a year that, while not a total disaster, was one that fell far below his expectations.

In 30 rounds in 1996-97, Scott had a 73.2 stroke average. In 13 of those rounds he shot par or under, including a 66 in the final round of the NCAA Championship at Conway Farms Golf Club.

Although he didn't win a tournament, he had four top-five finishes, including a second at the Puerto Rico Classic. He tied for 17th at the NCAA East Regional and tied for 20th at the national championship.

For the second consecutive season, he was named honorable mention All-America by the Golf Coaches Association of America.

But he expected more. So, too, did others, who often asked during the course of the season, "What's wrong with Steve Scott?" Scott heard the whispers. He tried to ignore them, but he felt the pressure.

As U.S. Amateur runner-up, he earned an invitation to the Masters last April but missed the cut. Three weeks prior, he received a sponsor exemption into the PGA Tour's Honda Classic in Florida. He missed the cut.

"You know people are talking, and what you end up trying to do is show them you can play," Scott said. "The only problem is, the harder you try the more you press yourself. I began struggling with my swing, and that didn't help matters."

When the college season ended, Scott finally said enough was enough. He worked hard on his swing, vowing to cast aside all the expectations and "just go out and play golf."

This past summer he won the Dogwood Invitational and was selected to the U.S. Walker Cup team, where he helped the Americans to an 18-6 victory over Great Britain & Ireland.

While he had a disappointing '97 U.S. Amateur — he failed to qualify for the 64-player match-play field — he's bringing a new attitude with him into the 1997-98 college season.

"There's not as much pressure on me this year," Scott said. "I don't think people have as big of expectations of me this year. And, while I still expect a lot of myself, I'm not going to put any pressure on.

"My golf swing is 100 percent better than it was six or seven months ago. It's more fundamentally sound, and I'm really looking forward to this season."

Florida coach Buddy Alexander knows Scott has the ability to be a top college player if he can keep control over his competitive fire.

"He's worked hard on his swing and has improved a great deal," Alexander said. "There's no question he has a solid game. What he's doing now is making every effort to control his emotions. He's so competitive and sometimes that becomes his downfall."

Scott's first test came last month when Florida opened its season at the Ping/GOLFWEEK Preview Invitational. He shot 76-74-71 for a 5-over-par 221 and tied for 39th.

A year ago, this would have sent his blood pressure soaring. This time around, Scott seemed to shrug it off.

"I just didn't play all that well," he said. "I'll go back and work on my game and hopefully be better prepared for the next tournament (the Jerry Pate Invitational Oct. 20-21 in Birmingham, Ala.). I've just got to keep plugging and not get down on myself."

To whom much is given, much will be required. *(Courtesy of Golfweek Magazine.)*

KARSTEN SOLHEIM

August 28, 1996

Steve Scott
c/o University of Florida, Men's Golf
P.O. Box 14485
Gainsville FL 32604-2485

Dear Steve:

Your fine play in the U.S. Amateur finals last Sunday had a great many people admiring your game. My wife and I were watching, cheering, and sending some prayers up, too.

You are to be highly commended for such fine play, and composure and effort that never faltered.

We look forward to following your career at the University of Florida. Good luck in your academics and upcoming tournaments.

Sincerely,

Karsten

Karsten Solheim

Mr. Solheim sent me a beautiful letter not long before he passed away. Perhaps it's best he never read what I wrote in this book about that three wood that almost abruptly ended the finals match. Mr. Solheim, it was a great three wood, just not so good off skinny, bent-grass fairways. *(Courtesy of Steve Scott.)*

Jack Nicklaus

February 12, 1997

Dear Steve:

Thanks for your recent letter. I apologize for not getting back to you sooner, but I have been on the road quite a bit lately.

I would be happy to have you join me for a practice round at Augusta on Tuesday, if you are free that day; however, I am not really sure what time I will play. I fly up to Augusta that morning, so it is usually late morning or early afternoon by the time I get to the course. If you will stay in touch with my office (Marilyn Keough) we can let you know more as my plans shape up.

I look forward to meeting you.

Sincerely,

Jack Nicklaus

I asked the great Jack Nicklaus if I could join him for a practice round at Augusta, and he said he would be happy to have me join him. I will be high as ten kites for the rest of my life about that one. *(Courtesy of Steve Scott.)*

I asked the '97 Open champion if I could play a practice round with him at Augusta, and he said yes. He could not have been any nicer—what a special day that was. To think I would play three straight practice rounds, all with major championship winners. Wow, just wow. *(Courtesy of Steve Scott.)*

February 11, 1997

Dear Steve,

I appreciate your letter, and of course I remember you. I have been able to follow your career a bit through the golf publications and have been quite impressed. The one piece of advice I would have for you is to follow through with your degree. Even though you will play golf for the rest of your life, it is an achievement that you and your family will be proud of. I know there are many people on the PGA Tour who wished they would have worked a little harder to get a degree. Enough about that, let's talk about Augusta.

In case you are unaware, any player that is exempt to The Masters is allowed to go any time during the year to play the golf course. This is something that was recommended to me by Tom Kite and Ben Crenshaw when I was an amateur, and I would urge you to do the same. I played the course about three weeks before the tournament, and it helped take away some of the awe of the whole tournament experience. Do not go there expecting the greens to be lightning fast, but it will help you get an idea of what to expect and what sort of shots you need to practice before the tournament. Just call the tournament headquarters and they will be very helpful.

I would really enjoy playing a practice round with you. I will be arriving on Sunday, April 6, but we can figure out the day and time later. In the meantime, my home number is 214-528-4413, if you have any questions. I will be traveling quite a bit during the next few months, but I check my messages frequently. I look forward to seeing you soon.

Sincerely,

Justin Leonard

Jack, Kristi, and me on the first green at Augusta. What an unbelievable honor to play Augusta with the greatest golfer of all time in a Tuesday practice round at the '97 Masters. Holy moly, and still a holy moly twenty-five years later. *(Courtesy of Steve Scott.)*

My Wednesday morning practice round with Steve Elkington and Greg Norman, the number-one golfer in the world at the time. It's the 9th green at Augusta. I don't think I made the putt, with my hands shaking like a tractor wheel plowing the fields with torrential rain on the way. *(Courtesy of Steve Scott.)*

Rolling down the hill on #1 at Augusta, my mind just blown and every piece of my being equally blown away by the fact I am playing in the Masters with my honey on my bag. I'm not sure if my feet ever touched the ground. *(Courtesy of Steve Scott.)*

Second tee box at Augusta. Wednesday morning practice round. Note everyone's expression. So, so, different. Man, I was so ready to set the world on fire. *(Courtesy of Steve Scott.)*

I played with major winners Justin Leonard and Bob Tway in my first and only spin through the Par 3 Contest at The Masters. Boy, that was a blast! *(Courtesy of Steve Scott.)*

I had seen these before, of course, but never one with my name on it. Note Kristi's caddie number: 26. My birth date is 7-5-77. Add up 7, 5, 7, and 7, and what do you get? *(Courtesy of Steve Scott.)*

I'm 1 under after 4 holes in the '96 U.S. Open at Oakland Hills, just outside of Detroit. My lead turns out to be a brief one but I didn't care. I can honestly say to my grandkids: Hey, your grandpa once led the U.S. Open! Told you the old man once had some game. Golf is a funny, funny game. *(Courtesy of Steve Scott.)*

Nineteen ninety-six, on a four-man team that included Hall of Famer Expos catcher Gary Carter! We won, somehow, beating Greg Norman's team by a shot, when Norman was the number-one golfer in the world. Crazy. No wonder we are smiling—in disbelief! *(Courtesy of Steve Scott.)*

I six-putt the last of the 54 holes. It's an eel-slick, twisting 50-footer, and I lose and finish 5th. If you miss a putt in this event, you must bring it back to half the length of the original putt length that you just missed. This is where my yips began. Had I won, I could have declared myself professional after the fact and won the first prize of $250,000. That darn 6-putt cost me 250K. Brother, can you spare a dime? *(Courtesy of Steve Scott.)*

To the victor belong the spoils. To the guy who six-putts the last hole from 50 feet, albeit a lightning-fast 50 feet, a 5th-place trophy. Putting guru Dave Pelz is doing the honors. *(Courtesy of Steve Scott.)*

The tournament committee paired all the US Am runners-up together. The fact that all three of us lost to Tiger in consecutive years is not lost on me. *(Courtesy of Steve Scott.)*

How crazy—we won the darn thing—that is, the Walker Cup in 1997 at Quaker Ridge in Scarsdale, New York. The whole shooting match. Boy, I felt like the sky wasn't just the limit, but the beginning. *(Courtesy of Steve Scott.)*

The 1999 Walker Cup Team in Nairn, Scotland. Our captain, Danny Yates, the boys, and me. Playing for our country. Pretty darn humbling. *(Courtesy of Steve Scott.)*

Kristi and me on the practice tee at the Broadmoor, in Colorado Springs. Kristi's sister was living there at the time, and we flew out for a little family visit and a chance for Kristi to peg it up in a high-end women's amateur event. Not sure of the result, but it was always so special just to be together. *(Courtesy of Steve Scott.)*

Golfweek/Titleist AMATEUR RANKINGS

Tiger turns pro, and I soon become the number-one amateur golfer in the world. The year before, I was number two. I'll let you guess who was number one. Sky's the limit, right? Well, sometimes the sky changes, but that's not always a bad thing. *(Courtesy of Golfweek Magazine.)*

Kristi, J.C., Kaylie, and me, walking proof that you can win in life without actually winning. *(Courtesy of Steve Scott.)*

That is my mindset.

If Tiger is going to win, he's going to have to do some miraculous things.

Think about it—if I win just one hole on the front 9; if I win the front 9 1-up, that puts me 6-up with nine holes to play. I'm going to win, simple as that. The match is over. Still, I can't help but think: how can I stop him?

ON THE FIRST TEE, OUR 19TH HOLE of the day, I have the honor. I stripe one down the left-hand side of the fairway—an 8-iron in; Tiger finds fairway as well but misses the green and short-sides himself. Not to my surprise, even though the pin is 23 paces on and a scant five paces from the right, Tiger hits this phenomenal flop shot to about twelve feet, which may not sound all that close, but considering what he was up against it's a hell of a shot. I make an easy two-putt and watch without expression as Tiger pours in his 12-footer as if it has eyes.

I later learn that commentator Johnny Miller said of that putt: "This is the first sign of life we've seen out of Tiger all day."

No denying it's a huge putt. He misses, and I go 6-up after nineteen holes. That's a bunch.

But Tiger doesn't miss.

We halve the par-three second hole, our 20th of the day. Both making fairly simple pars. On the 21st, the dogleg right par 4, with the tee shot a little uphill, I drive it into the fairway, left center, while Tiger blows it way, and I mean *way* right. Forty yards right of my drive if it's an inch.

This moment is depicted on the cover of the book you're holding in your hands. I'm walking off the tee as Tiger is walking on.

Tiger hits it so far out there, he only has wedge into the green; I've got 7-iron. The green is elevated, guarded by a creek. The pin is just back of center and left, and there are a lot of backboards and sideboards to take advantage of. I miss the green by just a touch before Tiger hits a tremendous shot in, using the backboard (much like the one on the front of number one green at Augusta) to roll his ball back to the pin, where it finishes a mere two feet away.

Heck of a shot.

I concede the putt, miss my chip—I didn't have a real good look at birdie, anyway—lose the hole, and just like that I'm 4-up instead of five.

Now, Tiger has the honor.

At Pumpkin Ridge, there are five par 5s, which is unusual for a championship course, and with Tiger's insane length off the tee—from the fairway, too—you think such a setup would play right into his hands, when in fact it's been just the opposite, at least so far. Of the five par 5s we played in the morning match, I win four of them. A bit of a surprise to me, and I imagine a shock to Tiger.

The trend appears to continue (though nothing in the game of golf is a given), as Tiger hooks his tee shot on this 22nd hole into the deep rough—has no choice but to lay up. I stripe mine down the middle, finding the greenside bunker with my second, which is fine by me. I love bunker shots; the sand wedge is one of my favorite clubs in the bag. Tiger has a wedge in from about 130 out for his third—hits it sky-high and one-hops it to two feet. Another kick-in birdie. Still, I like my chances. Up and down and we push the hole, and I'll still be 4-up.

I settle into the greenside bunker and dig into the sand with my classic leather FootJoys (which are heavy as southern guilt—nothing like the lighter-than-air golf shoes of today—but man, did I love those things, the leather, the Tungsten spikes) and choke down a touch on the grip and blast my ball out in what I think is the perfect trajectory and spin.

Unfortunately, it rolls farther than expected on Pumpkin's firm, fast greens. Not that the firmness and speed come as a surprise—I've had a hundred-plus opportunities to experience them firsthand this week, but still it's a touch unexpected to see my ball trickle by the hole a good ten, now twelve feet.

I know Ben Hogan famously said (more than once) good putts go in, but I'd like to think I hit a good putt there—it just didn't go in.

So now I'm 3-up and feeling a definite shift in momentum. No sense in lying to myself and saying I don't feel it. Kristi and I don't talk about it, though. Why would we?

Only thing to do is shift it back.

On the 5th hole, the par 3 and our 23rd of the day, where Tiger dunked two shots in the water during our morning round and just gifted me the hole, well, it doesn't fit my shot shape any more now than it did six hours ago. It's a left-to-right green, and with the pin fourteen paces on, the shot is right at 200 yards. I pull my 4-iron a little left, leaving myself a fairly long putt that I run by five feet. Tiger hits a solid 6-iron in (he's always two clubs longer than me)—doesn't stone it by any stretch—but it's an easy two-putt par.

My turn.

This five-footer suddenly looks like ten. It's a right edge putt, and I decel on it, and we all know deceleration on a putt of any length is almost always the kiss of death. If not death, it certainly dangles the mistletoe. I miss the roll a little low and, well, that was it.

Now I'm only 2-up, with thirteen holes to play.

This is exactly what Tiger needs and exactly what I don't.

What the heck just happened here? This isn't working out quite like I'd planned and it's happening way too fast. Boom, boom, boom. Cannons firing like in *The Hunger Games*. I'm leaking oil, not like seeping into the ground like the Beverly Hillbillies, but there's an undeniable trickle. A drip pan; drops of oil on the floor of your garage.

No need to panic and call the mechanic.

Still, I'm starting to feel the pressure, and it's mounting, which is exactly what Tiger is wanting me to feel. I'm sure he also wants me to feel doubt, but that's not how I'm wired. You may doubt me, Tiger may doubt me, but I will never doubt me.

Before the day ends, I'll card nine birdies and just three bogeys in thirty-eight holes. That's not bad, not bad at all.

In fact, that's pretty darn good.

If this had been stroke play, I would have won.

And if a frog had pockets, he'd carry guns and shoot snakes.

WORLDWIDE TV COVERAGE PICKS UP ON THE 6th hole, our 24th. No one tells us, but I can sense it. I know Tiger senses it, too. I say senses, because Tiger's hardly said two words to me all day besides "thanks" when I tell him "nice shot," or "good putt," which I say often on the second eighteen holes of our match.

So with the TV cameras rolling, the entire world is seeing what we are seeing. What all 15,000 fans here are seeing. And I gotta admit, knowing that feels pretty darn electric.

The sixth hole at Pumpkin Ridge is a dogleg left, 440 yards. I don't play it very well in stroke play, but it fits my sweeping draw of a drive like white gloves on Santa. Tiger finds fairway as well, and we hit almost identical shots in, both about thirty feet away from paydirt. Not really putts you expect to make, but you certainly don't expect to three-putt them, either. Neither of us does. It's easy fours both, and it's off to the next tee.

Sorta.

We both roll it up to about a foot and a half; I may be about three inches farther out. So Tiger is eighteen inches from the cup, and I am twenty-one. I concede Tiger's putt, fully expecting him to concede mine. I'm barely a business card outside of him.

Tiger doesn't concede my putt. Wow. Really?

Maybe it's because I just lost three holes in a row, and Tiger is wanting to get in my head like a Holiday Inn lounge-lizard hypnotist. Okay, fair enough. If that's how you want to play, then that's how we'll play it. Tiger, you're not getting into my head without a screwdriver.

I bury the gimme putt dead center.

Are those putts miss-able? Heck yeah, they are, especially when the tension is so tight, if it were guitar strings you could play Jimi Hendrix's Woodstock *Star-Spangled Banner* on it. But no way was I missing that one.

I was gonna fly backward to the moon before I missed that one.

I'm back in the game. *My* game.

Am I nervous? Of course I am. I've been nervous before to the point where the clubhead feels like a fistful of feathers, so light it could slip out of my hands at the next swing. But this is a good kind of nervous, the kind of nervous that means you are alive and in the absolute thick of the biggest moment of your life. At least up to now—when I marry Kristi some couple years later, that will become the biggest moment of my life.

And when our kids come along, the stage gets shared.

In the most life-changing and beautiful of ways.

ON TO THE 7TH HOLE AND OUR 25th of the day—the long par 5 where in the morning round Tiger hits a big snap-hook driver like an Indiana Jones whip crack, and I win the hole fairly easily, with a par as Tiger makes bogey. This time, Tiger hits his 2-iron stinger, which he does a lot, more often than not on the second eighteen of our thirty-six-hole match, because he wants to hit first into the green. To show me what he's got and put the pressure on me. And also, because he doesn't hit his driver worth a damn in the morning match, spraying it like a cat all over God's green Earth. (Tiger will later change this great swing that he thought was flawed that day—felt like he was across the line and shut at the top—with another great swing, after winning the Masters by 12 shots in '97 with said flawed swing that he felt wasn't good enough for him.)

You win the Masters by twelve shots as a PGA Tour rookie over the greatest golfers in the world and you change your swing?

But off the seventh tee Tiger hits a pure-as-spring-water 2-iron stinger right down the middle, 260 yards if it's an inch. The fairways at Pumpkin Ridge are firm, sure, but it's still quite a poke for a 2-iron. I hit driver past him, down the right-hand side of the fairway. The pin is nine paces on and eight paces from the left—a really good pin for me.

We both lay up—this par 5 is a good 600 yards and change, with a layup that just may be the toughest in all of golf. Sounds a bit crazy, I know. But it's narrow as a bowling alley. Ball-eating bunkers down the left, huge trees down the right. Tall as Augusta's legendary loblollies, I'll soon learn.

Because I have to start the ball flight so far right with my draw, I almost hit those monstrous trees, laying up with my 4-iron. But I succeed, and so does Tiger. We both have wedge into the green and leave ourselves somewhat makeable birdie putts.

Tiger has a birdie putt before I attempt mine, leaving it just short of the hole. Right in the heart, the ball looking into the cup like a cat into a fish tank with the lid off.

I don't scare the hole, slides a good foot right, but still it's an easy par.

We push the hole.

Bleeding stopped.

I'm still 2-up, going into the 8th hole, our 26th of the match. We both hit 2-iron off the box. It's a short par 4—385 yards, give or take?

This time, I'm hitting first into the green.

The pin is eighteen paces on, back left and on the back shelf, a tiny little shelf—elf on the shelf, this pin is. And I hit this beautiful 8-iron in. If you go over the green, you are absolute toast; if you hit just shy of the shelf, you've gotta putt up and over this hogback, and it's just tough.

Two-dollar-steak tough.

I hit a perfect little trap draw from 163 out, to just below the slope. I fly it 155, and the ball takes this one big, beautiful hop on the flat before the hill. The second hop hits into the hill and the hill kills it just a bit, and my Titleist checks and scoots right up there to about six feet right of the hole. I couldn't have hit it any better. Shot of the week.

Shot of my life under the circumstances? I'm thinking, *All right, Steve, let's get this thing back.*

I have a six-footer to go 3-up.

Tiger tries to do the same thing as me—land it just below the slope and hop it by the flag—but he puts too much spin on it. It hits the hill after the flat and spins down, thirty feet away.

He almost cans the putt. It burns the edge like a match on the lighting side of a good cigar. I concede his putt. I can feel the timing of this, and now it feels good. Really good. Get the match 3-up with ten to play. In good command of this thing that has gone awry.

THERE ARE A FEW PUTTS I WISH I would have had back that day—of course, there always are in any match, any round, truth be told— but this is one of them. Maybe and perhaps and probably this is the biggest.

Another right-to-left putt—funny how those putts drive me crazy when it's the exact same pattern I embrace from tee to green. I know this is a big putt, a huge putt. Not make-or-break, but definitely a deep bruise or laceration should I miss.

I go through my routine; I do everything I have to be me. But I get over the ball, and for some reason I will never know and still wonder to this day, I decel. Again. Just like I did on the 5th hole, our 23rd.

Aw, man.

Now, I am mad. For the first time all week. Straight up angry at myself, but I don't show it with clubs slamming or swinging. I'm as raw as cured bacon—just all internal. I am, however, some kind of frustrated. I'm hurt, and I know I've hurt myself.

I should have made that putt. The first time on that front 9 I could get one back on him. I had lost a few holes, and it was my one chance to put one in the win column. I gave myself a gift with that beautiful 8-iron to six feet, but for some reason I couldn't open it, in spite of how easy the ribbon peeled off into my hands.

That putt was huge.

Momentum is everything in match play, and that was my chance to seize it. Recapture it. But I let it slip through my fingers, like a hundred-dollar bill dropped from the sky, the wind blowing just enough to make it move left when I move right. Down to the ground it goes, like I'm Andrew McCarthy in the '80s movie *Class*. When he's on the rooftop with Jacqueline Bisset.

The next hole favors Tiger so dramatically it's not even funny. And I just opened the door that he is walking through, with a big ol' grin on his face.

Except Tiger doesn't smile.

The only time I see Tiger smile during our 38-hole match is on the practice tee with Butch Harmon during intermission and at the end, after he won, with his mom and dad.

Tiger has the honor off the next tee, our 27th hole of the day.

The 9th hole at Pumpkin Ridge is a dogleg left, a long par 4, 460 I think, and back in the day that could have just as easily been a par 5—with two school bus-sized bunkers in the center of the fairway. If ever a hole was made for Tiger, it's this one. Incidentally, this hole will become the first hole of the playoff.

Most tournaments go back to 18. This US Am will go back to 9.

Why, I do not know. TV, maybe?

To the bunker complex is 260 yards. I should have hit a rolling 2-iron to keep myself out of trouble, but I didn't. To carry that bunker is 300 yards—holy moly. Keep in mind this is 1996. Only airplanes can carry a golf ball 300 yards (unless you are John Daly, three bourbon and diet Cokes in and high as a kite, maybe two kites—but man, could John hit a golf ball).

But that is *exactly* what Tiger does—he just bombs it over God and everybody and those massive bunkers and has wedge into the green. I've never seen anything like it in my life.

Wedge, into a 460-yard par 4!

I have a 2-iron out. The way I've played the hole all week. My mind is a touch blown, I'm not gonna lie. I can't give up that much yardage to Tiger. So I pull out my 3-wood. Spur of the moment, but I am a bit of a mess after what I just witnessed.

That is one colossal drive.

There are two fairways for me to choose from. The fairway on the left is narrow as a grade-school ruler—maybe fifteen yards wide. The one to the right? Maybe forty yards wide, and a safer play, but you have a *much* longer shot in. Bunkers in the center are no good; you can't reach the green from there. If you miss it left, you've got a whole lot of nothing. Deep rough and huge evergreens blocking your path to the green. Mountains of needles and bark.

So I take out my Ping 3-wood and think: if I can pipe one down the right-hand side, I can hang. I've got a chance. Up and down to tie or win the hole? But my mind is so all over the place all the same.

I never get committed to a good target and block it way right. I'm in the rough now, with maybe 250 to the hole; so, so far right. I'm so far away from everything, including hope.

I'm 250 from the hole on my second shot if I'm an inch.

And Tiger, with a wedge in. I just spotted Tiger 100 yards off the box.

I take 2-iron and scoot it up to about fifty yards from the pin, but into the first cut of rough. Up and down for par is as good as I'm going to do. I have totally opened the door for Tiger to walk through however he pleases. No pressure whatsoever, and it shows when he hits his wedge shot twelve feet left of the hole from a rather tricky lie.

With the pin twenty-one paces on and just back of center, I hit one of my best pitch shots of the week to two feet. Tiger knows I'm going to make par. And what a par it will be.

I can feel it in the marrow of my bones.

Tiger walks up cucumber cool and cans his putt, accentuating the win with a fist pump. Not the full, uppercut fist pump—just the hand-raised version—but a fist pump, nonetheless.

Now, I am just 1-up with nine holes to play.

In the stretch of holes three through nine, Tiger picks up four holes. If you're thinking stroke play, Tiger just shot 33; me, 37. It's not like I gassed it, took a knee. And I will shoot 33 on the back. If you're still thinking stroke play, Tiger will shoot 65 in the second 18 holes of our finals match. Could have been 60, looking back on it, had he hit a few more putts a little firmer to the cup, instead of lagging and hoping I would make a dumb mistake.

I will shoot 70.

Tiger just played phenomenal golf. What else can I say?

WE ARE ESCORTED TO THE 10TH THROUGH the thick-as-thieves gallery of 15,000—the largest finals attendance in the history of the US Amateur—by Pumpkin Ridge founding member and coowner Gay Davis, who's done so much great work to get championship golf out to the Pacific Northwest, which is largely underserved by the USGA.

Built with the sole goal of one day hosting a USGA event, Pumpkin Ridge is just four years old at the time of our US Am dual in the sun.

22

THE SHOT OF MY LIFE

(CURIOUS—WHAT WAS YOURS?)

THE 10TH HOLE, OUR 28TH OF THE day, is a very clever par 3.

Tiger still has the honor, hits it up there about thirty-five feet left of the back-right pin, which is 21 paces on and just eight paces from the right. Tiger misses it (if you want to call hitting the green a miss) in the correct spot, doesn't short-side himself. He's in fine shape for a two-putt par at the least.

I'd won the 10th earlier in the day with a birdie 2, hitting 4-iron because the hole was playing a little longer than now because of the morning air. Rolled it up there six feet from the pin and canned it. This time I take 5-iron—perfect club for me, but I block it a little. I'm pin high, the ball a little above my feet, on a bit of an upslope, which some may call lucky, but I'm fine with that.

I'll always rather be lucky than good.

It's the perfect scenario to hit a flop shot. The lie is okay, sitting down a touch in the long rough, but not buried. It's also above my feet, quite conducive to the flop shot. I feel really good I can get a club on it, all the meat on the bone. It might have looked improbable to others, but it looked very probable to me. I love a flop shot, and I love my 60-degree Cleveland lob wedge. This looks more than probable. Might sound crazy, but it looks makeable. At least to me—lover of the flop shot that I am.

Turns out it is.

I land the ball exactly where I wanted to land it—Tiger is standing just right of my sight line of vision in an act of intimidation (something he still does to this day, by the way), but my Titleist is rolling pretty quick due to the downslope, and the pin just four paces off the edge.

Ok, it's motoring—no other way to say it.

It's also *tracking*, like my Titleist is iron ore and the flagstick a solid, metal beam. To quote booth announcer Dan Hicks as my ball dives into the hole like a ferret, "Steve's ball just had a wreck with the flagstick!"

Best I could've done there if it doesn't go in is twelve feet? Fifteen?

This is the first time the momentum has swung in my direction all afternoon—a huge shot in so many ways.

This bit is kinda funny. Wish I had thought of it as I was flying through the air with my legs tucked under like I was doing a cannonball into the deep end of a pool. Kristi wants to give me a high five, but I'm so pumped up I almost forget she's there. When the ball clangs into the hole, I jump into the air so high I could've dunked a basketball, even weighted down by my old-school, heavy, leather-soled FootJoys with the Tungsten spikes. The electricity that goes through your body at a moment like that is insane, when you have that much adrenaline flowing through you like snowmelt, and suddenly you're Mount Everest. The mountain I am trying so hard to climb.

When I land from my sky-high jump, it's a wonder I don't topple over backward, being on the upslope like I was. Not that I would have cared. Not after a shot like that.

I've never felt that much electricity flowing through my body, before or since.

I look directly at Tiger after I land. Come and get me, big fella.

At that moment, I honestly didn't think he could.

I just pulled a Tiger, on Tiger.

Kristi ends up slapping me on the back instead of high-fiving me, because my hand is nowhere to be seen. She will give me some good jabs about that over our years together, and we'll laugh about every single one of them. And I'll deserve every single one of them.

Her jabs, I mean.

23
TURNING POINT, MAYBE

TIGER MISSES HIS PUTT TO MAKE IT a formality, and we head to the 11th tee, our 29th hole of the day, with me, the decidedly under-dogged Steve Scott 2-up, the pendulum of momentum fully swung back on his side.

This US Am is mine to win.

I can tell that Tiger is upset, maybe a touch in disbelief. I can dig that—I am, too. That outcome is the absolute *last* outcome Tiger was expecting. What I *can't* tell is if his unhappiness of said outcome is a good thing, or a bad thing. For me, I mean. Internally. For the outcome of the match.

I'm about to find out.

I've got the honors on the box and stripe it down the middle, pretty much as good as I've got in me. Still, it's basic distance for the times for those who can rip one prerocket ball and springboard golf clubs—270 I hit it off the tee give or take, which is a lot longer than people realize. Especially when they go out to their local track and their ripped drives roll out to maybe 210.

Long for the average Joe, I am, but nowhere near for Tiger. *Holy moly* can Tiger launch it like Cape Canaveral.

Tiger gets up there and just pulverizes one—one of the biggest drives I've ever seen in my life. Flies my 270-yard drive by half a football field. Cutting a corner on this dogleg I have no way on God's green Earth of cutting with all the knives in the world.

It is an absolutely perfect tee shot on Tiger's behalf.

Second shot in.

There are two huge evergreen trees in front of me despite my pretty darn good drive, if I want to reach the green. I have to hit a little butter-cut shot, but I don't, and it flies fairly straight and lands pin-high, just left of the green. I still to this day don't hit a cut shot very well, but this is one of my best if I have a best in that category.

Perfect, in my eyes, though I know they are sometimes blinded.

I'm just shy of pin-high. Maybe six yards short of the green. It's a pretty easy chip to get up and down for birdie and maybe win the hole. First cut of rough, so it's fluffy, just enough cushion. I'm liking where I stand.

A lot.

I watch as Tiger cruises his next shot up and over this field goal of those crazy-tall evergreens, eighty feet if they're an inch—a 6-iron, I believe it was—but in the trajectory of a lob wedge. I kid you not. The ball was so high as it took off and the way it landed, holy smokes. It takes off Tiger's clubface like a hot air balloon, from two hundred yards out, and lands on the green as if Pumpkin Ridge's greens are suddenly soft as sandwich bread, though we both know they are hard as Christmas fruitcake.

Tiger takes a direct line to the pin.

If Tiger doesn't hit it that high with a draw, his ball is going to fall into a low collection area beside the green, where there is no way in hell he is getting up and down. But in true Tiger fashion, he pulls it off—draws it just enough to save himself.

It's kind of a blind shot what Tiger is up against, but he sees it with Superman's vision—an amazing, amazing shot.

Tiger's ball lands like a butterfly with sore feet, finishing 35 feet from the cup for eagle.

I'm chipping first because I'm still away. I gotta keep the pressure on Tiger, and I do, hitting my chip to just two feet away. A two-footer straight up the hill. I mark it. Making Tiger know I'm going to make birdie.

I'm *gonna* make birdie.

Tiger's got this putt for eagle, and it is dateline long. From where I am standing, it easily looks 40 feet. Pretty flat about halfway through the putt, then it goes up over a little mound and then back down it breaks hard left-right, a falling-off-the-cliff kind of break. A crazy-hard putt. All that is missing is windmills and a tiny creek made of cement and runoff, like something out of Putt-Putt at Myrtle Beach. It's one of those putts we've all faced before, that if you had a hundred tries you would miss a hundred times. More often than not, you're going to three-putt the putt Tiger is facing.

I certainly would put myself in that category.

If you have a hundred tries at it from where he is, you're not going to make it. This is one of those putts. So I'm thinking I can win this hole. I'm sitting right there for an easy birdie, the way I'm putting today. You are certainly not gonna put this putt Tiger has within six feet of the hole unless you bury it.

Tiger buries it.

Tiger hits the most perfect putt you've ever seen—certainly the most perfect putt I ever have, and I've seen a bunch, some even off my own flat stick.

When the ball disappears, Tiger puts on the full Tiger Woods fist pump like we have all witnessed so many times over the years. Arm to the sky like he's trying to punch out the clouds.

I thought his arm was gonna fly out of his shoulder socket.

His booming voice was loud as double thunder.

No one has ever pulled a Tiger on Tiger like I did on the last hole, when I holed out the impossible from the improbable. And now it is punch, counter punch, except Tiger's punch is a haymaker on steroids. You got me and now I got you, Steve Scott. And here is my fist pump for good measure.

You got your impossible and now I got mine.

Tiger stole that 11th hole from me, just like I stole the 10th hole from him. I forced him to pull out the greatest from within him. And he did. Wow. If I'm thinking percentages, before Tiger hit that putt, I'm thinking I win this hole a third of the time in this scenario, tie it most every time, lose it maybe one out of a hundred times—and yet I did.

I lost the hole.

Isn't life, and the game of golf, funny?

The 10th and 11th holes are of this match pretty darn epic. Finals match-defining. Tiger and I both pull off back-to-back miracles.

Now, I'm back to only 1-up, instead of what I thought was a very good chance to be three. One-up, with seven holes to play. I don't know if that is good or bad. Fewer holes to play, or do I want more? To have to control my own adrenaline when Tiger is feeding off me like a shark, as I go from bleeding to Band-Aid to bleeding again.

Tiger's rabbit came out of the hat like it was shot out of a cannon.

24

I AM ONLY 1-UP

HOLE 12 AT PUMPKIN RIDGE, OUR 30TH of the day.

Tiger has the honor.

The 12th at Pumpkin Ridge is a clever little short par 3. Over a pond, where a tiny green awaits. Slopy putts no matter where you stick it, not a flat spot to be found. If you are above the hole, you may as well be putting in your bathtub, trying to stop it short of the drain.

Hundred and thirty-two yards, although it plays every inch of it, which I know sounds funny when you're talking about such a relatively short distance.

Sometimes short can be a very long way.

The pin is in the front middle, five paces on from the front and five paces from the left. Tiger hits his shot about fifteen feet long and left of the hole. I know Tiger has a putt he must be a little defensive with. He doesn't stick it in there tight, doesn't blow me away with his shot. Takes a little bit of pressure off me, for sure.

It makes it a little easier knowing your opponent has a defensive putt.

There's a fan in the gallery, not sure who he is a fan of, who yells out as I start to swing: "Hey, come on, *Steve!*" and I back off my shot as I respond with, "Hey, come on, *fan.*"

I didn't take it personally. I'm in a really good state of mind, despite just taking an uppercut to the jaw moments prior. The great thing, one of the many things that are so great about match play, is that each hole is like its own minitournament within itself.

Once a new hole begins, there is always hope.

I hit my wedge up there—a little trap draw, which you know I love to hit. Put the ball a little farther back in my stance to try and squeeze an extra four or five yards out of the shot, which I can't physically hit otherwise. Keep the spin down, drive it in a little lower. Nine iron is too much club—I've got to keep it below the hole, or I am toast, with the pin just five paces on and five from the left.

There was no such thing as a gap wedge back then.

I don't quite hit it as well as I want to, and it ends up on the front edge of the green. But it's an easy putt, one I can roll up pretty close. Eighteen feet, maybe twenty. Not one you expect to make every time, mind you, but certainly two-putt.

Which I do.

Tiger has a slippery roll downhill—defensive, like I mentioned. A left-to-right breaker. He puts a good roll on it but doesn't convert.

We halve the hole. A little back-to-Earth moment after the last two epic holes. I am still 1-up, with six to play. As every hole gets you closer to the finish and you have the lead, you start thinking, "Hey, can I win this thing? Is this really gonna happen?"

It starts becoming a little bit more real as you get close to the finish line.

IT'S A SURREAL MOMENT ON THE NEXT tee, the 13th, our 31st of the day. Par 4, the pin front left, just twelve paces on of a thirty-nine-deep green. Not a long hole.

What makes the moment surreal is the amount of people surrounding us. The space between the back of twelve green and thirteen tee, where people walk down to get to the fairway, has been trampled on quite a bit during the week. A light breeze is coming in from the right. The fans, the gallery, what looks like all fifteen thousand of them, have kicked up quite a bit of dust and dirt. It's like when the fog rolls in through the trees and the sun shines into it, separating it into fragments. The beginning, or end, of a tornado.

Like the Carl Sandburg poem about the fog coming in on cat feet in San Francisco. Straight off the bay.

This was off the back of a tee box.

I've never seen anything like it. This Pumpkin Ridge track wasn't built for huge crowds, yet there are 15,000 trying to find their way.

So am I.

Tiger has the honor and stripes his stinger 2-iron, and I do the same, but with my driver. Tiger hits first to the green, wedges it to about 25 feet on the fairway side of the hole. I've got wedge in, as well—pretty much the exact shot I had on twelve, almost the exact same distance.

Another trap draw dialed up.

The pin is front-middle-left, and any shot four or five feet past the hole will go down into the lower portion of the green. The front of the green is kind of high, the middle half of the green kind of low, which is a little unusual. *Unique* might actually be the better word. You don't see that very often in golf. In fact, I can't tell you of another green like it.

I hit my wedge a little too hot. When it lands just past the pin, I know exactly where it's going and go it does before stopping about thirty feet from the cup. Three quarters of the way it's uphill, last bit it goes flat, almost runs away a touch. It's not an easy putt by any stretch, especially with the tension in the air, so tight you could play the bass line in *Another One Bites the Dust* on it.

I roll it a good four feet past the hole.

Tiger lags it up, damn near holing it in the process. I quickly concede his putt before it changes its mind and goes in.

I don't hit that great a putt on my next one—looks like it's going to break below the hole before my Titleist suddenly grabs the bottom corner after almost circling its way around the cup and spins into the front of the cup and disappears. One of those putts that kind of sneak their way in, like you might into your bedroom window in high school before sunrise after you snuck your way out at midnight. Lucky, no doubt about it.

But as I said before, I would rather be lucky than good.

We head to the fourteenth.

I'm 1-up with five to play, still very much alive.

Fourteen is a short par 5 up a proper hill, a walk you'll feel in your thighs by the time you reach your drive, the fairway sloping upward like the back of Sasquatch. Favors a right-to-left shape. So many holes at Pumpkin Ridge favor a right-to-left shot. It's unbelievable, really. It is as if this course were made just for me, designed by the architect Bob Cupp with me in mind.

The fourteenth hole is no different—a dogleg right to left, fairway bunkers down the left. Tee shot is up, second shot is down. You hit up to a plateau, second shot down. There's a tiny pond, short left of the green, but just big enough to pull a *Jaws* on your Titleist and swallow it whole. Green is tiny, like the pond—maybe the size of a backyard pool in a middle-class neighborhood?

I know those well.

The green is only 22 paces deep, one of the shallowest greens on the course.

We both find the fairway off the tee, with Tiger hitting 3-wood and not his 2-iron stinger, past my driver. I have 190 to the green, but it's downhill, and I hit 6-iron. On-course announcer Roger Maltbie tells the world I hit 4-iron, but Roger is just guessing. It's not like he went over and looked in my bag.

I hit a great shot, which finds the front of the green and releases to about fifteen feet from the hole where I've got fifteen feet for eagle.

This is so needed. I needed to let Tiger know I wasn't going to lie down like—and no offense—all his other finals US Am opponents have lain down in the past. I was not going to go away quietly.

I firmly believed I wasn't going away at all.

Incredible comeback be damned.

Tiger tries to dial one in, but his phone goes rotary, and he floats it about four yards shy of the green, setting up a 60-foot chip shot. Fourteen green runs away from you a touch, a little bit front to back. Tiger's chip shot runs out a bit more than I bet he expected, to about six feet past the hole. He didn't hit it that hard, but it just kept rolling and rolling.

Man—just so, so fast, these Pumpkin Ridge greens. Announcer Johnny Miller says they are the fastest USGA greens of the year, US Open included, a tournament he won back in the day, shooting 63 in the final round at Oakmont.

I believe him.

Still, Tiger's chip makes me go: Hmm.

But as soon as I hit my putt, I know it's a miss—so close, but you know when you know, and it sneaks right along the edge and rolls by a foot or so, a gimme. Tiger concedes it.

Birdie 4.

Tiger also misses his putt for the up and down. Backs off it, doesn't look comfortable, comes back to the moment, but he misses. Pulls it a touch. It's just the second hole I win in the afternoon part of the match.

The fifteenth hole awaits.

So now I am 2-up, with four to play.

In match play, at least in my eyes, holes 13, 14, and 15, so close to the end, are really huge holes. If you can turn the momentum your way—for instance like in my case, get 2-up with three to play—how can you *not* win?

In a lot of my previous matches I really turn on the jets on hole 14. I win this hole a bunch. With birdies or pars while my opponents fall apart around me.

Why, I do not know.

But that is where it *has* to happen. That stretch of holes. If you are even going into 14 and you lose two holes in a row, you are two down with three to play. But if you *win*, you are two up with three to play, and that's a hard one to come back from. So those holes, when the match is really tight, are so important— the magnitude is insane. You simply cannot lose them.

I get the honor back.

I am back in control of the match.

The next hole, fifteen, is a straightforward par 3, maybe 185 and change?

I have a 5-iron in hand—Kristi clubs me, just hands it to me, no discussion; she's great at that when it matters, and boy, does it ever matter right now, and I hit it pin high, a little into the wind. The pin is just off the left edge of the green, five paces. There is a spine in the middle of the green—a hump, and it's right in my way.

What the caddies at Augusta call a hogback.

I have a 30-footer for birdie. Tiger hits it closer; I imagine he has a 7-iron in hand, and he just stones it—leaving a really good look at birdie. Twelve feet, maybe?

I almost make my 30-footer. *Almost* is a great word and a terrible word all at the same time.

My speed control is really good on the greens at Pumpkin Ridge, my nerves intact. All week long. Still, this is the most nervous golf I have ever played in my life. But this is exactly why everybody plays golf, same reason people parachute out of airplanes: for the adrenaline rush that feels so incredible, even though it's painful. An adrenaline rush like this gives you these superhuman powers, allowing you to do things you normally wouldn't be capable of doing.

There is no better feeling in life than hitting a great golf shot under pressure.

Against Tiger Woods, who is trying to make golf history, a history I am trying to rewrite. Not many people make history as an amateur. Bobby Jones is the only one who comes to mind.

One person, out of literally millions.

My putt rolls to a stop, barely short, call it half an inch, but a miss, nonetheless. But I force Tiger to make his putt. Or else, we tie the hole.

Tiger misses. We tie.

I'm still two up with three to play, and I have the honor. This is really good. I'm thinking if I win this hole, this 16th hole, our 34th, I win the US Amateur. This match is *over*, baby. But as you know from earlier this morning, the pin is all the way in the back-right corner of the green, and I can't fade the ball to save my life. I am still so nervous—but it's a good nervous.

I can win this thing. I can win the US Amateur.

Kristi is beside me, all smiles and shoulder rubs and back pats. And always the right words at all the right time. Kristi can talk me off the ledge of doubt and fear like nobody I have ever known.

I go through my routine with my driver, pipe it down the middle a good 280. Considering all that is hanging in the balance, it's my biggest drive of the week, and that's saying a lot. Tiger gets up and just absolutely destroys one. According to on-course announcer Roger Maltbie, he's 53 yards past me.

So, Tiger just hit his drive 330? He has 120 in, and I have 171. We also have very different angles into the pin, which explains the yardage into the green for both of us. But I get a bad break.

Like broken arm bad.

My 280-yard drive lands in an old divot. Filled in, but a divot, nonetheless. Topped with dirt but hollow beneath as far as solidity goes. In the midst of being healed up, though sitting down below the ground that surrounds it, but still, a bad lie.

A bad break at a bad time.

My swing is so in-to-out because I hit a sweeping draw, as opposed to being a fader, so my angle of attack into the ball is shallower than I need for this lie. Nobody's fault but my own. This is just who I am.

I *must* go steep into this shot in order to expect a good result. I physically cannot get down to the ball like this moment requires, try as I might.

I hit a kind of chunk shot to the right.

Not a good shot, considering I was in the middle of the fairway, albeit in a dang divot. I float it into the same bunker I'd been in during the morning match. But I'm farther back. I'm not on the upslope. Much, much harder shot.

Tiger has a sand wedge into the green, with me in the right-hand side bunker, lying two. Tiger's sitting pretty as Snow White. I'm one of the Seven Dwarfs—which one, I don't know.

If you do, don't tell me.

This is a pin you can get really close to if you have a lie anything like I didn't.

25

THE SPACE BETWEEN

WITH A NOD TO THE
DAVE MATTHEWS BAND

PRIOR TO WHAT IS JUST ABOUT TO happen on this life-defining hole, our 34th. The moving of the mark back reminder, I mean. Okay if I say a few words before we get there?

To the moment that changed the game of golf forever.

I've blasted out of the bunker to about 10 feet from the cup. Kristi has looked at the putt before me, like she always does. Asks me what I see— "What is the speed are you sensing, Steve? What is that slope going to do to it?" Kristi points. To that slope running off the edge of the ridge of the green.

"The grain is running like a greyhound toward it, honey. Do you see that?"

That's how good Kristi is.

She gets my mind from emotions to calculating when the situation calls for it, as it does now, like a long-distance call from the moon.

I know I must make this putt—a huge putt at the time: match-changing at the least, life-changing at the best. If I don't make this putt, I'm giving Tiger the hole. A gift. Merry Christmas. I know I must focus with all of my being. And I am so, so nervous—my heart jumping through my blue-and-white-striped Tommy Hilfiger shirt like it's playing leapfrog with itself with my shoes. I can feel it beating, and I can *hear* it beating like a tom-tom. I wonder if Kristi can hear it, too. If I were to guess, I would bet she can.

Kristi knows me that well. Better than I know myself.

I am just that nervous.

It is an amazing feeling. It's not a *great* feeling, because you've never had your heart beat that fast before. But still—

It is an amazing feeling. Even my eyeballs are throbbing. I try to blink them down to calm.

There has been so much adrenaline running through my body all day that it should have blown the skull off the top of my 19-year-old head. And I'm so nervous at the same time, trying to muster up the focus and to strike a putt the perfect speed and hit the exact line you have to hit, and hope you and your caddy, your girl, your best friend, guesses the break just right.

What a conglomerate. All while you are shaking in your FootJoy boots.

It's really pretty mind-blowing how you can make a putt, any putt, from under that amount of pressure. Look at how you can miss in so many ways.

Look at Scott Hoch, at the '89 Masters in his playoff against Nick Faldo on the 10th. A three-footer to win, and he blows it four feet by. Scott was cross-grain, and it was slicker than a wintertime rooftop, but still. Scott made the comebacker—which was pretty darn impressive, though he was never the same again after he lost on the 11th instead of donning a Green Jacket on the 10th.

Scott Hoch pretty much disappeared after that.

Then there's Ed Sneed, also in the Masters, when he lost to Fuzzy Zoeller and Tom Watson in a three-way playoff. Ed left that little four-footer for par on 18 in the final round hanging on the lip like fat over a belt buckle to win outright.

There is a great photo (although Ed may not think so) in that year's *Masters Journal*, of Ed standing over his ball, head hanging down and just a wishing it in. It really is hanging on the lip something fierce. If a drop of rain had landed on it, it would have fallen into the hole.

One more: Doug Sanders in the 1970 British Open. Doug's putt was hardly longer than the length of his colorful shoes. I am a big fan of Doug Sanders, by the way—loved the way he dressed. Loved the way he played, carried himself. A great ambassador for the game was Doug Sanders. He was also a fellow Florida Gator, and winner of the 1956 Canadian Open as an amateur—the only amateur to ever do so, and the last amateur to win on the PGA Tour until Scott Verplank in 1985.

Doug had some major game, but I think maybe he had too much fun on and off the course to end up being just very good, and not great.

And the physical shots that turn mental—Chip Beck laying up (when he absolutely *had* to go for it) on the par-5 15th at Augusta, in steady second place—three shots clear of third but two behind leader Bernhard Langer with just four holes to go. Chip was never the same again. Chip's layup shot even bounds over the green.

Chip caught a lot of hell from the media for laying up when

the moment called, no, *screamed* for him to go for it. So what if you don't clear the pond? At least you could say you tried.

Sadly, Chip misses 90-plus cuts after that and is soon gone from the Tour.

There's also Ray Floyd dunking a 7-iron into the pond on 11 from the middle of the fairway in his Masters playoff against the aforementioned Nick Faldo. This, from the guy who once set the tournament scoring record at Augusta. Ray, too, disappears.

Grievous mental errors beg mentioning, as well. Roberto Di Vicenzo in the '68 Masters signed an incorrect scorecard— he signed for a *par four* on the 17th instead of the *birdie three* he made just fifteen minutes earlier—to lose the tournament by one. In tournament golf, you are only responsible for your score on all eighteen holes, *not* the total score.

Broken confidence is a bone that never heals. It bears repeating.

Broken confidence is a bone that never heals.

MY CONFIDENCE ISN'T BROKEN BY ANY STRETCH, but at this moment I am so nervous I can't feel my hands. They are jitter-bugging beside my pockets like crazy. It's hard to believe I can muster up the courage to do what I have to do.

And I have always played golf fearlessly.

To hole such an important putt when you must do it at this moment, at this time, well, it's just . . .

Sounds kinda crazy, but it's like a biathlete—where they have to ski down a crazy-sloped mountain and then shoot a rifle at a target in the distance the moment they get to the bottom.

In golf, you have to just stand there. You can't just go and take your adrenaline out on someone, like in hockey, knocking a defender into the boards. You have that same amount of adrenaline flowing through, but you must subdue it. You must get yourself in a state of mind to allow you to perform these delicate acts.

While your body is on absolute fire. To have the wherewithal to make that putt, and after I make my putt, to see what I see next—I don't know where that golf world-changing wherewithal comes from.

The game of golf itself?

But if I *don't* make my putt, I concede Tiger's. I give him the putt.

And none of this even matters.

Think about that for a second. I think about it almost every day.

Well, not every day. I've got a wife and two wonderful kids. They take up most of my thoughts and time, and I wouldn't trade that for the world.

But if all of these crazy stars hadn't aligned. If I walk off the 16th green another way. If Kristi wasn't in a certain spot off the edge of that green with the bag. If I hadn't turned my head at just the right time.

The list goes on and on.

As does life.

26

DEFINING MOMENT

(BUT AREN'T THEY ALL)

THE 34TH HOLE.

I'm standing on the 16th tee, so nervous. My guts are spinning like the *Price is Right* money wheel. I get up there with
my driver, pipe it down the middle a good 280. Considering all
that's hanging in the balance, it's my biggest drive of the week,
and that's saying a lot.

Tiger absolutely destroys one, a good 53 yards ahead of me,
as per on course reporter Roger Maltbie. That's a long, long
way in golf. I'm hitting 6-iron in; Tiger, a pitching wedge. For
most of the second 18, Tiger doesn't take driver, hitting that
2-iron stinger he will soon become famous for.

Man, that thing can travel.

We are both looking at our pin sheets. The green is 38
paces deep, and the pin is 30 paces on and 6 paces from the
right. There are some side boards. If you take it a little back of

the pin, you can spin it back something serious. Which Tiger does, but he does it out of the rough.

I block my approach shot out to the right.

My game is built around a ball that spins more than the golf balls of today. Drawing the ball right to left. My fade is really a block, and into the right-hand side bunker I go. Same bunker I was in in the morning round. I have almost the exact same shot, but this lie is worse. The morning round she was sitting up nice, and I almost holed it.

Tiger three-putted the hole in the morning round, to lose it.

Tiger hits this towering wedge into the first cut of the rough just behind the green, where it lands and, well, should stop. But it one-hops backward *out* of the rough and spins back down to six feet for a very makeable birdie. Just a phenomenal shot, for the ball to spin like that out of the rough.

Out of the *greenside rough*. Tiger's ball spins back down the hill perfectly, as if tied to a choreographed string.

Only he could do that.

I didn't shake my head, but, man, I wanted to.

My lie in the bunker is sketchy, sitting down a bit, and a quarter of the ball is nestled in the sand. Imagine your ball sitting in beach sand, the soft bit farthest from the water—no way to get good spin on it. I have to carry about twelve feet of inclined bunker—don't think for a second I wasn't thinking about my bunker shot on the 17th last year against Buddy Marucci, where I got too cute, left it in the bunker, and lost the hole.

I blast it out best I can, but my ball lands a little on the downslope and rolls ten feet past the pin, directly on Tiger's line, four feet beyond his mark. Unless I holed it, ten feet was about as good as I could've hit it. If I had tried to cut it any closer, I could just as easily keep it in the bunker as clear the lip. That is a chance you just can't take.

Not in that situation.

Tiger's mark is right in the way of my par putt. I point to Tiger's ball and say, "Hey, Tiger, can you move that one to the right?" And he does.

I know I need to gently float my putt right over where his ball mark is if I'm going to make it. It's a slight left-to-right break if I remember correctly. I do remember we had the exact same putt, with mine being a few feet longer than his.

I ask Tiger to move it one lower than the break, one down. Knowing I absolutely must make the putt to put on the pressure, or I'm just gifting him the hole.

Kristi and I are looking at it, eyeing it up.

Kristi gives me a great read that I believe in. I swear I can still hear my heart beating through my cotton golf shirt, but somehow, I bury the putt, or maybe God buries it. A huge putt. One of the biggest putts of the day for me.

The biggest putt of my life?

It's really amazing how you can make a putt under that amount of pressure. You get so nervous you can hardly feel your hands, and you're having to make a putt of this magnitude on greens rolling 13 on the Stimpmeter, with TV cameras rolling and the massive gallery of who all but a handful of the 15,000 (that would be my aunt and uncle) are pulling for you to succeed.

It's hard to believe you can muster up the touch and the nerve to focus on making such an important putt at a time when it's truly make-or-break.

Oddly enough, in the morning round, on the exact same hole, I hit the exact same approach shot. But then I damn near holed my bunker shot, my lie in the bunker much better than now, with my Titleist Professional 100 doing a complete horseshoe around the hole. Tiger 3-putted for bogey, and I won the hole.

Even *that* was rolling through my mind as I struggled to gain control of my shaking hands and racing heart. But I was so, so focused on that ten-footer with everything hanging in the balance like bats in a cave.

After all, if I don't make that improbable putt, none of what happens next matters in the least. And there is no story to tell.

As I AM WALKING OFF TO THE side of the green, after taking my ball out of the hole with still trembling fingers, taking seven or eight steps *after* I take the ball out of the hole, I see Tiger setting up his ball behind his mark. I'm halfway between the hole and the side of the green, looking out the corner of my eye. No idea as to why I'm looking out the corner of my eye at Tiger. I haven't done that all day long.

It's like I've been called to do it.

Not enough time, Tiger.

The timing in my brain says there was not enough time for Tiger to remark the spot, to go through the process of locating the landmark he used to move the mark in the first place (was it a tree? Edge of the bunker I just blasted out of?) and correctly move his mark back to its original position.

I'm like, wait a second.

It was instantaneous.

It was like lightning went through my body—the same lightning that flowed through me at 7:15 a.m. on the first tee. Instinctual. Just that quick.

It came to me that quick. It was never should I do it or should I not?

It was just a "Hey, Tiger, you gotta move that back." It's just what you do in golf. At least the way I play the game.

Here's the thing.

When you a play a tournament that is seven days long, your ability to focus becomes amazing. You are going through these automated motions. Your routine is so automated at that point. You've hit all these great shots under pressure—bad shots too, of course. It's like you're in a trance-like state, where you are so focused on the job at hand, and each moment, hitting the shot, going through your routine, and how you are going to navigate the big chess match that's unfolding on the golf course.

All the things that everybody else is thinking about, you don't have time to think of that stuff. All you're thinking about is what is going on in the match. How can I hit the shot to put the pressure on the other guy?

Johnny Miller even said it on the telecast. He said it was rule of thumb in the game of golf, to do what I did.

The stakes are so much higher now—so, so much money to be made through endorsements, Tour prize money. Maybe someone else wouldn't have done it. That's not my call. But for me, it's what I did, and knowing that I did that will always give me a clear conscience of what happened next.

I guess I did it for golf. It's just what you learn, what I learned from Ray, who never charged me a dime for a lesson, and my dad. Golf was always there for me. It was always there for me, my best friend when I had no friends, and, in a way, I needed to be there for golf. This is something I have thought about often—almost every day of my life ever since.

I never thought I was going to write a book about it, though. Feels cathartic, oddly enough.

It's the parallels, I guess. Why we do things as people.

AT THAT MOMENT, WHEN I TOLD TIGER to move his mark back—well, it's why I love the game. And maybe that's why it loved me back, a lot. But that moment is why I needed to be there for golf. A lot of times, you don't get out of golf what you deserve, but sometimes you do—but in that realm, that moment, it was the right thing to do for golf.

Golf was always there for me.

I needed to be there for golf.

27

"LET THE LEGEND GROW"

TIGER DOING TIGER THINGS

THE 35TH HOLE.

I'm still leading, one up with two to play. Still leading, but in a way, make that many ways, it feels like I'm not.

Tiger has the honor.

Tiger hits his stinger 2-iron off the box—his stingers fly low and they stay low, like a heron grazing tidal marsh waters, like hood-of-the-car low, and those stingers run for days, and I hit 3-wood, just a little past Tiger's stinger.

We both find the fairway.

Tiger hits 6-iron in, blocks it a bit, right side of the green. I'm thinking, *if I can win this hole, it's over*. The whole thing is over right now. It's a left-hand pin—a very comfortable pin for me.

I just barely overhook it, the wind coming in from the right a little bit—an aggressive play, but I'm going in for the kill. I see the opportunity. Tiger is 40 feet away from the cup.

I certainly am not expecting him to make that birdie putt, a 40-footer and change.

Foolish me.

I end up just off the green with my 6-iron, pulling it just a hair into a tricky lie in the rough. Bluegrass rough, and because of the way the grass lies, it's sticky, like fingers after a summertime popsicle. I'm only twenty feet from the hole. There's a side slope, downslope. Not too hard to get it up and down, but a very difficult shot to *make*. To hole it. Which I've done more than once this week, and if I can do it here, well, I win the US Amateur.

When I get to the green, the air changes. The energy. I can feel it in ways I've never felt before. I can feel it through the air from the gallery, as if they are willing Tiger's ball into the hole.

Kristi feels it, too.

It's the strangest thing ever. I walk to the side, off the green, to a little mound to get out of his sight line, although he loves to get in mine, and I see Tiger make his putt before he even lines it up. I see it happen before it happens. I see it happen in my mind, the way you might see the trailer for an upcoming movie at the Regal Theater.

In match play, you always expect your opponent to make his putt. But not this one. This thing is a 40-footer.

But I see Tiger make this putt, in my mind's eye, before I even hit my chip shot.

Plain as day.

I know that sounds crazy.

For a long putt, it's a fairly easy putt, if there is such a thing for a 40-footer. But there was like a trough to the hole—you hit it a little left, it goes right, a little right it goes left, but this putt is moving, cooking, hauling ass. If Tiger's ball doesn't hit the hole, it goes an easy eight to ten feet by.

It could've lipped out, but Tiger's putts don't lip out; they always lip in, I kid you not. No, this putt hits the corner of the hole and gets sucked in like the hole was attached to a vacuum cleaner at the local car wash with the ON button on permanent hold. No more tokens needed.

It's like Tiger's will overpowers any gravitational force.

And, well, that was it.

Just like that, I've been punched in the solar plexus. It's all I can do not to go down on one knee. The momentum has most definitely shifted. Kristi tries her best to, as she likes to say, get in the way of the momentum vibe, the vibe that has just gobsmacked me on both sides of my face. And Kristi does, as only she can. If she isn't there for me at that moment, the match would have been over right then and there.

Tiger and I are all square, for the first time in 32 holes. I won the third hole of the match and never trailed, until the very end, when he beats me in the playoff. Tiger never *leads* the entire match, until he beats me.

This defies all logic.

All square, going into the 36th hole.

28
ALL SQUARE

How are we possibly all square? after all I have done to make it otherwise.

I do not know, but we are.

Hole 36.

The eighteenth at Pumpkin Ridge is a dogleg left par 5. Fits my shot-shape perfectly. If I hit two good ones I can reach. Tiger and I are all square, all tied up like a granny knot. We haven't been tied up since the third hole in the morning round.

Tiger and I have gone 33 holes with me either all square or leading like crazy.

Like 5-up crazy.

What the hell has just happened?

Let it go, Steve, let it go.

Eighteen at pumpkin ridge is a bit of a weird hole. If you don't hit a really good drive, can't carry it far enough, there's an environmental area you have to lay up short of, but if you carry the environmental area, on your second shot, you only have 100 yards into the green. Give or take. I knew if I hit a good drive, I could get pretty close to the green. But there's a hazard all the way down the left-hand side. Hit it in there, and you are toast without the butter. If you hit it hard left, you're going to have to retee.

It's a do-or-die tee shot, this one, no question about it.

Tiger hits first; he has the honors after that unbelievable green-in-two putt he just made.

Tiger hits this massive power fade, on this dogleg left par 5. He sets up down the left-hand side, hits it over all of the hazard area, aiming *over* all the trouble, and peels this gorgeous fade back over into the fairway (who does that?), which I think is beyond amazing. Towering, like an airplane taking off with me looking out his window seat. And Tiger has hit his driver terribly all day—maybe four times he has found the fairway? When I saw the driver in his hands, I thought: *This could go right into the spinach and the match is essentially over.*

But it didn't. It went right into the heart of the short grass.

The best drive I have ever seen in my life.

Now I am supernervous once again.

I know I have to hit this fairway, have to give myself a chance to go for the green. I know Tiger is going for the green, has a great chance for birdie—even eagle. I give it my quick little buggy-whip swing, and I draw it into the fairway as well, albeit not as far. I'm about 280 to the green—Tiger is 240, probably less. But I am in play. I'm also spotting Tiger 40 yards on the deciding hole of this epic match. And he hits it 40 yards past me at will. Hell, I'm not spotting him 40 yards; I'm spotting him 80.

Tiger has 2-iron to the green and I've got 3-wood. I don't think I can reach the green, and I've got to clear another one of those environmentally sensitive areas that are indigenous to Pumpkin Ridge to get anywhere near it. And then you are still maybe ninety yards out. So, I have to fly it a good 200 yards just to be safe.

No big deal, right? Piece of cake.

I have this old Ping Zing 2 3-wood, very curved on the bottom, which is great off a tee but terrible off a tight lie, which is what these bent grass fairways always are. This Ping Zing 3-wood doesn't sit flush with the turf at all. No offense to Karsten Solheim, but this 3-wood is just an awful club for hitting off the deck. I don't know why I even had it in my bag.

But I did, and it was all I had.

I chunk the shot. No other way to say it. While it's in the air, I'm thinking it's going into the hazard.

I thought I lost the tournament right then and there. I thought I lost the tournament with just one swing. I worked so hard all day, and to lose it like that?

As the ball is in the air, it's half the trajectory of a normal 3-wood. I'm puckering, my heart sinking. As I see this ball at its apex, I know it's over.

It's not over.

By some miracle, my ball clears the hazard and runs up into the first cut of rough.

The reeds of the fescue are so tall they cover the other side of the hazard, where the grass starts again. I can't tell where it lands, but I do see it bounce, and golf balls don't bounce when they land in hazards. My ball literally clears by a yard, I'm later told, and not one that has a house in the middle of it.

It's the luckiest shot of my life.

I probably should have lost the tournament with that swing.

My worst of the day—the week. Green light for Tiger, yellow light for me.

Tiger's got 2-iron in, lying one. And he knows I'm 100 yards out, lying two. Tiger is licking his chops once again. There are these giant evergreens bookcasing the fairway. You can't hit it over them; they are like huge soldiers guarding the green, machine guns at the ready. Marines, first line of defense.

Tiger pulls it just enough to make me breathe again. Had he been six feet more to the right, he's got a very makeable putt for eagle. Fifteen feet tops.

The 18th green at Pumpkin Ridge is narrow—skinny might be the better word—with a huge collection area low to the left, and a tight chipping area.

It's a pretty damn demanding shot.

Tiger hits his shot.

If Tiger's shot is two yards right, he's fifteen feet for eagle. But it falls into the grassy collection area. He's got a tough chip, not much to work with. If he doesn't get it on the green, it's going to roll all the way back down to his feet. There is a collection drain in his way, as well.

I hit my wedge onto the green out of the rough—no chance for much spin out of that lie, can't really put any control on it—up to 25 feet, keeping it right of the hole. I have a downhill putt on these downhill mountain slick greens, breaking about a foot and a half right to left.

I have 25 feet for birdie to possibly put this thing away.

Tiger has a collection drain in his way, so he can't putt it even though the lie is Twiggy skinny, as is his path to the hole. He hits a very conservative chip to 12 feet. Heck of a shot even if it doesn't sound as such. If he had mishit in the least, it would have rolled back to his shoes. He might have even had to jump out of the way.

I blow my putt by five feet, barely missing on the low side. So, so fast, these greens. Augusta fast. I walk over, mark my ball, and step aside.

I'm thinking Tiger is going to hole his putt to win. Bring on the fist-pump and bring me right down with it.

But Tiger lags it up, thinking, I guess, that I am going to miss my comeback putt. I think that turns him defensive. His ball rolls up to about six inches from the hole, and I give it to him. He then puts the onus on me.

I have a 5-footer straight up the hill to tie the match and send it into extra holes. The 1996 US Amateur has come down to sixty inches of Pumpkin Ridge real estate.

And I am shaking in my FootJoy boots something fierce.

I'm also working on reserves. But one thing in my mind to send it into extra holes was from the year before. A lot of things happening right now come from the year before.

My brain is on fire, thinking about the semifinal match with Buddy Marucci when I holed the downhill sliding three-footer to send it into extra holes.

This is a do-or-die moment.

Obviously not die in the sense of die (though maybe part of your confidence could. Would? Should?). If I miss this putt, I lose the last three holes to lose the US Amateur 1-down. This will be very hard to live with. Tough pill to swallow. A *Jagged Little Pill*, to quote the great American-Canadian singer Alanis Morissette.

I have never had a pressure-packed putt like this in my life. There is such a finality to this putt. If I miss it, I'm done. I lose it all right then and there. I feel like I'm suffocating, gasping for breath, although my lungs are working quite fine, and no one knows what I'm feeling but me.

And Kristi.

Then something crazy happens.

As I'm about to hit the putt, going through my routine as I've done all week—much quicker than I do these days; perhaps I should go back to it—some small child or baby cries. And when you play in these kinds of events, you hear everything and yet you hear nothing. I hear the noise, in my *conscious* mind, but I make the putt with my *subconscious*. I tell myself how I'm going to make the putt. Like the devil and the angel on your opposite shoulders. Like in the movie *Animal House*, the devil saying, "I don't know, Steve. I think you're gonna miss this one," and the angel saying, "Nothing but net, Steve. Remember the downhill slider you made just last year against Buddy Marucci to send the match into extra holes?"

The angel's voice drowns out the devil's.

I've never been there before, in that state of out-of-body being, at least certainly not like this, and I've never been there since.

I watched myself hit that putt, out of body, from up in the clouds somewhere. I watched it roll off the putter head and into the hole.

About five seconds later, that is exactly what happened.

I wish everyone who has played the game of golf could one day have that feeling. It is burned into your mind, like a branding. The sizzling iron burning onto your arm, into your heart, into every piece of your being. To rise to the occasion, overcome the mental demons, mental nerves and hurdles, and the pressures of the moment.

My five-foot putt slides into the hole dead center.
Splits the 90-degree line of the 360-degree circumference.
That Titleist 100 golf ball would have rolled into a thimble.

29

PUSHED INTO A PLAYOFF

ALL THE WORLD'S A STAGE,
AND WE ARE MERELY PLAYERS

AFTER 36 HOLES, WE ARE GOING BACK to number 9, the most difficult hole on the golf course for a shot shape like mine.

God has a great sense of humor. He knows I can't hit a fade to save my ass.

Number 9 at Pumpkin Ridge, of all places—the worst hole for me and the best hole for Tiger. He has a huge advantage over me here. Center line bunkers that I can't carry, but he can. He can fly it over, and I have to lay up short. Tiger will have wedge into the green if he carries those bunkers. Damn the luck.

The rules official comes over and says we can have a bathroom break. We haven't had one, the whole second 18, now that I think about it. So why would I want to take a whiz now? We are drinking a lot of water, but don't have a lot to show for it because it's so, so hot. Even though it's Oregon, the air cool and crisp in spite of the temperature.

After the bathroom break, I go back to 9 because it's the first hole they have a TV tower on, I guess. I hop in a cart with Kristi and our driver—about a 500-yard ride or so to the 9th tee box.

The 9th is a par 4, the 10th a par 3, the 11th a par 5. That would allow them to mix up the different pars for our playoff. Maybe that's why they did it. I couldn't figure it out, as at the US Amateur, where Jeff Quinney won at Baltusrol, they go back to the first tee for the playoff.

TIGER SLOW-PLAYS US, NO QUESTION ABOUT it; he stays in the bathroom a long, long time. Looking back I know exactly why.

Tiger wants me to get out there first—to think about it. Think about what the hell just happened to me.

Felt like I waited there for an eternity, and Tiger with the honors. He's hitting first. So, of course, I have to wait. I can't go, and I am so ready to go.

But wait I do.

The cameras are on me pretty good—as we are waiting on Tiger. Kristi is giving me a back rub, telling me I can do this. I got this. She's so great, my Kristi.

Tiger finally shows up, rolls up to the tee like a red Corvette, and without so much as a hello absolutely crushes his drive. Absolutely smokes it. Hundred and thirty yards to the pin. I take out my 2-iron—I have to lay it up—it's a split fairway, only maybe fifteen yards wide, but if you miss it left you can't get to the green, and there are these huge evergreen trees. Like a tunnel, like I said. But you have *got* to be in the fairway.

It's 260 to the bunker and 300 to carry it. A reach I can't cover. A bunker Tiger flew like a *Blue Angel*.

I hit my trap draw 2-iron that flies 215, and it runs out to maybe 240. The bent grass fairways at Pumpkin Ridge are very firm. Hard as pool tables. Perfect USGA setup. The grounds crew, the superintendent, did a phenomenal job, I must say. The golf course was as immaculate as any golf course I have ever seen.

And I've played Augusta.

I spot Tiger 80 yards off the tee.

I have 207 to the hole, and I decide to take 5-iron, after talking with Kristi. It doesn't feel all that great coming off the club, truth be told, but somehow it feathers its way up to about fifteen feet from the hole. Pin high, and pressure right back on Tiger.

Tiger hits a wedge in, pulls it just a little bit—just a touch outside of my 5-iron.

This validates that you have got to play your own game, how it fits you, and see how it works out in the end.

Tiger has about twenty feet, I've got maybe fifteen. Five-iron, versus wedge.

These are pretty straight putts, just a touch downhill, a little outside left, pretty flat. We are both equally licking our chops.

Tiger misses, it just doesn't quite break the way he thinks it's going to break, and it finishes just left and past the hole. And I concede it.

Here's the moment.

After the whole entire day, ten-and-a-half hours of golf that started at sunrise and is about to end at sunset, and all the time I was 5-up in that morning match, and yet this is the first time, the only putt I've had to win the tournament.

I miss the putt.

Maybe I tried too hard. I don't know.

I miss it short, and a little to the right. A weak, right effort—I decelerated on it a little. Had I had one other putt to win, before that, I think I would have been a little more prepared for that moment.

Tiger concedes my miss, which I appreciate.

We go to the 38th hole. The 10th, the par three, a hole I had won twice that day. Even though it was a right-hand pin, and me with my sweeping draw. There was something about that hole I just liked.

Tiger hits a 6-iron and I hit 5. It is the first swing of his I watch all day.

I'll back up a second.

Tiger hits the ball so mightily high, and the greens at Pumpkin Ridge are hard as pool tables. It's an apex like nothing you've ever seen, how Tiger hits it—his ball could have flown the tallest tree imaginable—a high, glorious fade that comes down maybe seven feet behind the hole. Drops down like a butterfly with sore feet that just got burnt on the grill.

Tiger gives it his famous fist pump from the tee box.

I have never seen that before. Or since.

Who fist-pumps on the tee box?

After the insane tee box fist pump, I get up there and hit 5-iron, a great number for me, but I push it ever so slightly. I'm actually closer to the hole than I was when I hit the flop shot into the cup for a 2 during the second 18. This is a bit of a difficult chip, though, the way the ball is sitting down in the rough, on the downslope, with the green running away—I can see the quarter top of it.

I hit what I think is a great pitch—the ball lands just over the rough, onto the cut of the fringe, spinning just so, and rolls down to about seven feet. Just about the same distance of

Tiger. It's so close we have to call the head rules official over, Trey Holland, to call it. To tell us who is away. It's that big a moment. If I get up there and hole the putt first, I put the pressure back on Tiger, like the heaviest of blankets, forcing him to make. If I miss, Tiger has two putts from seven feet to win the US Amateur.

At first, Trey eyeballs it and says, "Steve, you are away."

Tiger asks him, "Are you sure? I think I am."

How does he possibly know?

Tiger asks for the measuring tape, and they measure. And it turns out Tiger is away by maybe a quarter of an inch. It's a crazy-fast putt he's facing, so I know he'll have to be defensive.

Tiger doesn't hit a great putt—he overreads the break, and it rolls by about a foot or so.

So now the stage is back on me.

All the world's a stage,/And all the men and women merely players.

Shakespeare, and Rush, wrote and sang it best.

I have the same pressure putt I had on the 36th hole. However, this one has a little left-to-right break on it. Not the ideal putt for me—would have loved to have it a touch straighter, or even right-to-left. I love straight putts.

I decelerate again, just a fraction, and I lip it out on the low side; it could've gone in just as easily as it stayed out. One of those slow, tantalizing lip-outs that just melts your heart. It melted mine like the Wicked Witch.

Maybe today really was like *Wizard of Oz*. I guess it just wasn't meant to be.

I don't concede Tiger's putt; I make him make it. But he makes it dead center, and well, that's the ball game.

IT TAKES TIGER A GOOD FIVE MINUTES to come over and shake my hand as I'm standing there, even with my hand extended as soon as he taps in, my hat off, at this point.

I put my hand back in my pocket, as the next scene unfolds.

30

AFTERMATH

I'M STANDING THERE, ON THE GREEN, WITH KRISTI. She has her hand on my shoulder. I should have my hand on hers as well, but I don't know where it is. My hand, I mean.

Tiger's dad, Earl, rushes over and gives Tiger a big, long hug, tears in his daddy's eyes. Tiger's mom, Tida, comes over; Butch Harmon comes over, everybody is hugging and crying on Tiger. I am just standing there. Like the last little kid at the day care center, waiting to be picked up by Mom or Dad.

I don't think the Tiger of nowadays would have left me hanging like that. The Tiger of today would have shaken my hand right away. Cap off, acknowledgment.

Great match, Steve.

There is an interview of both of us by Roger Maltbie after the smoke clears, the three of us on camera. Roger—who I think does a great job of interviewing players when they are on the spot, certainly not an easy thing to do—has been there before, having won on Tour a few times. Roger is a good dude.

Hard to imagine two golfers in the world higher or lower than Tiger and I are right now.

Strange to feel so low and so high all at the same time, but I'm not disappointed. In the outcome, sure, but not in myself. I did everything in my power to win.

I'm quite pleased with myself, odd as that may sound at a moment as broken as this. I could have folded like a cheap suit, but I didn't.

It just wasn't meant to be.

THERE'S AN AWARD CEREMONY FOR THIS 1996 US Amateur on the 18th green, just like there are at the British Open, the US Open, the PGA, and kitty-corner to the 18th at the Masters, by the practice green. There is a table set up with the Havemeyer Trophy for the winner, a gold medal and a silver medal close by.

I'll let you guess which one is for me.

I speak first, thanking the Pumpkin Ridge staff for putting on such a great tournament, the superintendent for a perfectly conditioned golf course, the fans for bringing such energy, and Tiger for being such an incredible competitor. What a match it was.

I hand over the mic.

Not once—and by not once I mean zero times—does Tiger reference me. Not once does he say it was a great match, that I was a great competitor, opponent.

Not once does Tiger say, "Hey, thanks, Steve, for telling me to move my mark back on the 34th hole. I owe you one, man."

No acknowledgement whatsoever of what I did.

It's like I don't even exist, as Tiger takes the microphone. And talks. About himself. Looking back, I just don't think

Tiger knew any better. I'm not laying blame on him for doing what he did. Tiger was born to be a cold-blooded assassin, and as much as he was on our second 18 and into the playoff, it continued at the awards ceremony. Acknowledging your opponent for his great play, to look outside himself for just a moment, was simply not hard-wired into Tiger's being.

During the awards ceremony, Tiger keeps going on about how Portland, Oregon, has been so great to him—he wins his third straight US Junior Am there and now his third straight US Am there. That's phenomenal. And I get that. After all, I would be talking about it, too. But there would have been at the very least an acknowledgement of my opponent and the great battle he brought to the table.

Of all the lessons Tiger learned growing up, he missed out on this very basic, but oh so important, one.

31

MATCH PLAY VS STROKE PLAY

SOMETHING'S MISSING

IF, AND I KNOW IT IS A *BIG* IF, but if my match between Tiger and me was stroke play, I would have won, having shot 68–70: 138 to Tiger's 77–65: 142. I reflect on this as I am writing this book, as I am watching the presidential election debate on the TV in our den.

In that '96 US Amateur, I win the popular vote but lose the electoral college.

Still, I lose the '96 US Am.

But—a loss is a loss, and I am okay with that, and, well, you must move on, no matter who you lose to and no matter how you lose. And that's cool. All good, but what I want you to take home is this: there is an undeniable connection between the two of you, player vs player, win or lose, in match play.

There is a connection between your caddies, as well.

There is an undeniable connection when you spend four-plus

hours on a golf course with someone you have never met before in your life. In the finals match, make that ten hours. It's as undeniable as a rusty razor cut on your cheekbone when you are a half-awake and trying to hurry into work.

Do you mind if I wax on briefly about the difference, at least to me, between match play and stroke play?

Some twenty years later in life, I'll host a big golf tournament as the head pro for The Silver Club Golfing Society—a 36-hole event that culminated an entire season of stiff competition. The first time I host this championship event, the finals are stroke play, everything to the bottom of the cup. It ended well, everybody happy and smiling, but to me it just felt like something was missing. And I honestly didn't know what that something was. But I did know it was a big something.

That changed this year, 2020, oddly enough. Match play across the board, start to finish. And the funny thing is, the whole *mood* changed.

In match play, you are going at each other, teeth bared; you know there can be only one winner, one loser.

But that also makes it so otherworldly intimate. And you want it to be played in the spirit of the game—two gentlemen playing the game as hard as they can. Knowing that there is going to be a final result at the end of the match, unlike stroke play, when you know there will be three more days to determine the outcome. But at the same time, as you traverse the course, you get to know each other. It's like you become friends overnight, even though years of life have separated you.

It's a battle, but there is also a connection. A special connection. You know there can only be one winner, and there will be one loser, and you both will know your place. Two gentlemen, or gentlewomen, playing golf in the spirit of the game, as it was meant to be played. There will be conceded putts, there will be honors on the tee—sometimes you, sometimes him or her.

When you concede a putt to your match-play opponent, there is a certain respect that you have for them. And there are certain times in a match where you might *not* concede a putt, like you might at another point in the match, depending on how the match is going.

Show me what you got, my friend.

There is a lot of interesting human interaction in match play that doesn't happen in stroke play. The only person you are playing against in match play is the only person that really matters.

Think about that, for a second.

The other person you are playing against is the *only* person that matters. There is a mental freedom you have in match play; each hole is its own individual entity, its own individual tournament. There are eighteen tournaments, in one round of match play. You open the door to another chapter every time you step up on the box.

You finish that hole, you close the door, and then you open the door to the next one. There is no looking back. And now you are in another room. It's like you are in a bubble.

A bubble, of newness.

It's very intimate, match play, boutique you could say, even though in my finals match with Tiger there were 15,000 people watching us up close and personal. And of course, the millions watching on TV. But at the same time, there is just the two of us.

Match play is one on one, instead of one vs one hundred fifty-five players like on the PGA Tour, or in the case of the US Amateur, one vs 311.

All that said, each hole that you play, in match play, is its own chapter, as the book of your match unfolds. That is what match play is all about.

But, at least to me, when the smoke clears, it's all about the connection between you and your opponent, the chapters as the matchbook unfolds, and the open and even the closed doors that bring you together.

For better, or for worse.

Like marriage.

32

THE AIR POPS OUT OF THE BALLOON

THE LONG EXHALE

THE ADRENALINE IS FLOWING FOR SO LONG through your body if you make it through all seven days of the US Am. Flowing like a flooded Nile River, and you feel like you are about to explode. It's like a week with your in-laws—even with the ones you love, and who love you back—the good times, the bad times, all times.

Which I do.

Love my in-laws, I mean.

But, yeah, the air popped out of the balloon. Our hot air balloon. Kristi's and mine. Hot air gone, lift force and weight no longer the same. Flame turned off and down you go crashing to the ground, though no one gets hurt. We just bounce into the bunker and into an unplayable lie. Time to get back into the rental car and go home.

I don't have to be on edge anymore, to deal with the pressure, the moments, the colossal moments. Still—

Damn.

Damn.

There are no tears, not at all, oddly enough, even though maybe there should be. But there *is* an odd relief of pressure. You can see it in my face, afterward; you can Google it. Kristi and I are simply relieved.

But don't get me wrong—I was crushed. Like an empty beer can at a fraternity party. Throw me away.

But.

I'm really proud of myself, crazy as that may sound. I stood up to the pressure; plus there was the 34th-hole thing, which, unbeknownst to me, will get a lot of attention as time goes by.

I'M SITTING IN THE BACK OF OUR Chrysler rental car, my aunt and uncle in front, Kristi right beside me, knee to knee, and I am looking out my rolled-down window, my mind racing like Mario Andretti's. It's quiet, like snow falling on cedars (by the way, the title of a great novel by David Guterson).

I knew how tough Tiger was going to be. I knew what a beast he was, going into that finals match. I knew what was coming—I just didn't know it would come that way.

Tiger has gone to the final hole of each one of his finals matches, be it the three US Junior Amateurs or three US Amateurs, needing to win that final hole to win the championship, or to push that match to a playoff, which he wins every time. I should find solace in that, but I don't. At least not right now, not at this moment in time. But the fact is that I hit so many tough shots, great shots, on TV and in front of the entire world, with all those fans watching up close and personal. I pushed Tiger to a brink he had never known before. And in the end, he pushed back, with a force mightier than any I had ever felt or experienced, and over the ledge I went.

But my hat is off to Tiger. It was, and will always be, the comeback for the ages. You have got to give credit where credit is due. I left *nothing* out there, that day at Pumpkin Ridge. Nor did Tiger.

There was nothing left in the tank for either one of us.

I have drawn on that unforgettable day at Pumpkin Ridge a lot, even in my everyday life, in so many positive ways over the past 25 years. The only negative is I didn't win that day. I did everything else the way I should have done it. Even on the 34th hole.

I guess I wasn't supposed to win.

I guess I played the role I was supposed to play.

33

THE 1997 MASTERS

AFTER THE MATCH, I GET A TON, and I mean a ton, of fan mail, which surprises me. I have never had fan mail in my life. Humbled the heck out of me, truth be told. I felt like I should have been sending fan mail back to *them.*

I go back to college for my sophomore year, and I get a lot of invitations for PGA Tour tournaments in the spring. Some I have to turn down, like the PGA tournament at Harbor Town, and a European Tour event at Loch Lomond, as both coincide with college team events, and I'm committed to my team. There are a ton of interviews, as well—I'm even on the front cover of *Golf Digest Japan.*

How crazy is that?

So incredibly humbling. And in some ways, disturbing. Not disturbing like someone peeking in your bedroom window, but disturbing like someone is peeking into your life as you walk down the grocery aisle at the local BI-LO.

I just want to be a kid.

THAT FALL, I AM INVITED TO PLAY on the World Amateur Team. Yowzah. We fly to Manila, in the Philippines, for the World Amateur Championship in a quest to bring home The Eisenhower Trophy, where we finish 9th out of 47 teams. There are only four of us on the team: Joel Kribel; Jason Enloe, who will go on to coach at SMU; Jerry Courville; and myself. Pretty wild to fly halfway around the world to represent your country.

God bless America.

In March of '97, I'm invited to play in my hometown Honda Classic, a Tour event I grew up watching as a kid and dreaming about, which is pretty darn cool. A nineteen-year-old amateur playing in his hometown event, paired with Stewart Cink, who will go on to win the 2009 British Open at Turnberry against Tom Watson, and also a chap named Frank "The Blade" Lickliter, who would one day lose the Buick Invitational at Torrey Pines to Phil Mickelson in a bizarre playoff. Double bogey 6 beats triple bogey 7 all day long. Or, as Ray used to say, "Don't tell me how, tell me how many."

I get a lot of traction out of not winning the '96 US Am. Perhaps the most notoriety of any US Amateur runner-up in history.

It's surreal playing in a PGA Tour event. The energy that is out there—everything that surrounds it—knows no bounds. It is luminous and voluminous. It's so much more than golf. There's so much going on; it takes a long time to get used to, actually. I'm not sure I ever did; in fact, I know I didn't.

It's like the Super Bowl, not once a year, but every week.

I PLAY A PRACTICE ROUND AT AUGUSTA, in March, the month before the Masters. The golf course is nothing close to what it is tournament week, as I later come to learn—still, I am blown away. And by that, I mean the pace of the greens. That said, the difference between Monday and Thursday of tournament week is like different time zones, America to Australia—so, so different. The ball doesn't roll back into the pond on 15 on Tuesday if you spin it off the green, but on Thursday, after the greens have been rolled and brushed and rolled again, it'll roll back into that pond like a bowling ball rolling down a roof line.

The week before the Masters, I peg it up in a college tournament, The Carpet Capital Collegiate in Dalton, Georgia, at a golf course called The Farm. Sweet track, great track. I drive separate from the team, because I'm driving straight to Augusta for the Masters as soon as I putt out on eighteen on Sunday.

My wheels are wounded—I'm kicking it in an old, beat-up, gold-colored Honda Civic hatchback. My Mazda RX-7 with the double subwoofer from the high school days is just a broken-down memory.

After our college tournament, I zip down to Augusta and pull into the front gate right around nine o'clock Sunday night, the moon having swapped places with the sun. Magnolia Lane—the dream drive of any golfer's life.

It certainly was for mine.

I could have died and gone to Heaven right then and there.

The guard stops me—there is a Smith & Wesson on his hip. He looks at me kind of funny, looks equally funny at my beat-up Honda Civic. I tell him I'm Steve Scott and I'm playing in the Masters.

The guard looks at me like that has *got* to be the world's biggest impossibility!

The guard asks for my ID, looks it over, and reluctantly lets me through the gate. Down Magnolia Lane I go. I'm not sure I even press the gas pedal. Just let my piece of nothing Honda roll down Magnolia Lane at her own pace.

Wow. Just, wow.

Doug Mauch, the assistant pro at Augusta at the time (and someone who I am friends with to this day), greets me with a warm smile and handshake and escorts me to my quarters: the famous Crow's Nest, with stairs like a ship's ladder, perched right above the pro shop. The stairs go straight up and straight down. You can see it from the 18th tee box—the Crow's Nest, not the stairs, of course. The line off that tee is actually the third window to the right. It's surprising to me—no one is staying up here but little ol' me. Tiger has turned pro, so obviously he's no longer an amateur; the US Mid-Amateur champ from Cali, Tim Hogarth, isn't staying there; and the British Amateur champion, Warren Bladon, isn't there.

Feels a little weird, having the place to myself.

The Crow's Nest is kind of like an Ivy League boarding school dorm room. Old school, with twin beds partitioned off by a nicely painted piece of plywood. There's a common area and a simple bathroom. But to know that you are staying on the grounds of Augusta National Golf Club, and you're playing in the Masters the next day. I wouldn't care if I was staying in a lean-to!

I'm playing in the Masters. Seriously? Is this real?

It's like Christmas eve, and I'm six years old again. I want to go to sleep, need to go sleep, but I can't. I don't toss and turn, just stare out into the half-light of that third Crow's Nest window, not believing my good fortune. Not believing I'm here, honestly. Me, Steve Scott, playing in the Masters.

When my alarm sounds—the one in my head, not the one on the clock—after maybe 5 to 6 hours of sleep, I shower, get ready, don some Tommy Hilfiger duds, carefully roll down those steep Crow's Nest stairs to Augusta's dining room for breakfast.

Which is something in and of itself.

There are no menus in the men's grill—the waiter walks up and you just tell him what you want, and the chef makes it for you on the spot. Like you are the king of the castle. Never experienced that before, or since. And everybody is just so, so nice. They treat me like I'm a member, my Green Jacket draped over my shoulders like James Brown at the end of the concert, and not some punk college kid from Florida driving a beat-up, gold-colored Honda Civic with lots of miles on the odometer and tires bald as Kojak.

After an amazing breakfast in the men's grill, I register for the Masters in a small white building just to the right of the pro shop. My player's number, the number Kristi will wear on her caddie's uniform, is, oddly enough, 26, a very special number in my life. My first date with Kristi was November 26, 1994. My brother's football number was 26. I carry a quarter and a penny in my pocket—26 cents—whenever I play. Unfortunately, the finals of the US Am were August 25th. Who knows? If it had been the 26th, things might have turned out differently.

After registering, I head over to what they call the east practice tee—opposite the main practice tee, right of Magnolia Lane if you're looking north toward Washington Road. It's a great little setup with a sloping practice green as fast as any on the course, surrounded by bunkers, with sand white as eggshells. I start chipping, and one of the gentlemen in white jumpsuits—a caddy helping out on the range, I'm guessing (I later learn it's longtime Augusta National caddy "Bull," personal caddy for then-current Chairman Jack Stephens, who will work the driving range during the Masters for over 25 years)—walks over and asks if my car is the beat-up Honda Civic over on the side of the clubhouse, not too far from where I'm chipping.

I tell him, "Yes, sir, that's mine," and he looks at me serious as a downhill three-footer for the win and says, "Boss, you gotta get that piece of shit outta here."

I don't know whether to stifle a laugh or call a tow truck.

I freeze.

And then Bull asks for my keys. Says, "I'll move it for you. Just give me your keys. But Boss, she has got to *go*."

I reach into my golf bag like a kid looking for a certain candy in his Halloween bag.

I PLAY MY MONDAY PRACTICE ROUND WITH British Open champion Justin Leonard.

Kristi, who left straight from a college tournament in Miami and arrived at 3 a.m., rolls in. She does not miss a beat. After a ten-hour ride from Miami, I sure wouldn't be happy about carrying my golf bag up and down the massive hills of Augusta after a night of no sleep. These are the highest elevations in golf from tee to green that I know of. From the 18th tee box to the back tier of the green—from the valley in front of the tee to the back of the green—is 11 stories.

Eleven stories.

That is one tall building.

AFTER MY PRACTICE ROUND WITH JUSTIN, I go looking for my car, and lo and behold Bull hands me a set of keys to a brand-new snow-white Cadillac, with the Masters logo bold and beautiful on the driver's side door. The Cadillac courtesy car is mine for the week, while my gold Honda Civic holds court in the caddy parking lot, where Bull took my keys and moved it; she is sitting pretty atop the gravel, weeds, and cigarette butts.

Right where she belongs.

Crazy, how I go from a beat-up Honda Civic to a brand-new Cadillac with eleven miles on the odometer. Eleven miles! The distance from the dealership to the course. The juxtaposition is not lost on me.

The next day, Tuesday, I have a practice round date with the legendary Jack Nicklaus, thanks to the suggestion of my University of Florida coach Buddy Alexander, who had the idea for me to write letters to anyone I wanted to play a practice round with. Keep in mind this was before emails and the World Wide Web were the norm. Write the letter, lick a stamp, and hope for the best. At Buddy's urging, I write letters to Justin Leonard, Jack Nicklaus, and Greg Norman, and they *all* oblige with a practice round, which I thought was very cool.

Beyond cool, actually.

On Wednesday, it's Greg Norman, Steve Elkington, and me. Crazy.

But not quite as crazy as what follows.

I'm standing on the west practice tee, hitting practice shots after my Tuesday round with the great Jack Nicklaus, still smiling and shaking my head at Jack's amazing read of my 30-foot birdie putt on the back of 9 green—I swore it was breaking six inches left to right, but Jack said, "No, Steve. It breaks six inches right to the *left*." Maybe that's why Jack has six green jackets and I have none. (For the record, Jack was right—I buried the putt for birdie.)

There is a weird buzz in the air, like when your hair stands on end and lightning suddenly strikes a little too close for comfort. Two-time US Open champion Lee Janzen is just a few spots away from me on the practice tee. He sees what I see.

I'm hitting 5-irons, maybe 180 yards out, give or take. About halfway through the apex of the shot, the ball does something really weird—it wiggles in the air, like a jingling bell cat toy with the feather on the end of it. Never seen anything like it. I see this little funnel cloud gather to the right of my ball flight, pulling up magnolia leaves from Magnolia Lane and into the air. This funnel cloud makes its way down the driving range straight to us—a few hundred yards if I were to guess. It's no longer little—forty feet tall maybe? Pretty much high as the net at the end of the range. A whirling dervish. It passes right by Janzen and me, and onto this footpath behind us that takes you back to the clubhouse.

And right as it reaches the clubhouse of Augusta, it evaporates. Like it never even existed. Even the magnolia leaves disappear.

Like it was the ghost of Ben Hogan, saying hello then good-bye, one last time (Hogan would pass away that July). Everybody on the range looks at one another with the same expression: "Oh, my God. Did you just see that?"

I know I did.

To this day, I don't know where it went. I do know this: it simply disappeared.

It is wednesday night after the Par 3 Contest, the night before the Masters tournament proper, and I'm staying in a rental home, hardly ten minutes from the course. It's a really nice place, huge—six bedrooms twice the size of mine back home, with lots of space to stretch out. My aunt and uncle are there, as well as Kristi, my dad, and my brother. My mind is racing with thoughts of the Par-3 Contest, where I played with Justin Leonard (again) and former PGA Champion Bob Tway, who holed out from the bunker on 18 at Inverness Club back in '86 to beat forever snake-bit Greg Norman by two. Turned a potential playoff into party over with one swing of the sand wedge.

I hit it to a foot on number three, my highlight of the day, but someone later aces it, so no crystal for me. But that's okay. The Par-3 course at Augusta is like the greatest thing ever. So much fun to play, every hole like a smile. If there is golf in the afterlife, it is the Par-3 course at Augusta. Heaven on Earth, or maybe it's Earth on Heaven.

I'VE GOT AN EARLY TEE TIME on Thursday, paired with '79 Masters champion Fuzzy Zoeller, so I'm up at the crack of dawn, the sun creeping into the sky as I pull out of the rental home driveway. It's cold out, too, at least it is for this Florida boy, with temps in the low 40s. The course is playing exceptionally firm and fast—imagine bent-grass greens on an airport runway.

We introduce ourselves and tee off. Fuzzy is nice as he can be. It is not lost on me that I am playing on Thursday with a former Masters champion. He really is so damn nice.

I remember walking down the 10th hole after hitting my drive down the right-hand side and it trickled beautifully into the flat, and I ask Fuzzy, casually, how he did in his first Masters, as we are making conversation, just shooting the bull, and Fuzzy turns to me and smiles and says, "Partner, I *won* my first Masters!"

Fuzzy was so great. Funny as all get out. Like playing 18 holes with your favorite stand-up comedian. One-liners out the wazoo.

Tiger, paired with two-time defending Masters champion Nick Faldo, shoots 70 in his first round (40–30—some kind of impressive, that). I carve a lousy 78, followed by a 79 on Friday, after being paired with former PGA Championship winner Bob Tway. I forget what Bob shot.

I miss the cut by a long shot. Call it a slingshot. With Augusta National, David. Not sure who was Goliath. Either way I was, as the Augusta caddies call it, Magnolia. Meaning I was about to haul my butt down Magnolia Lane on Friday, two days earlier than my hoped-for departure. Funny moniker, looking back on it.

The greens at Augusta are just *so* firm and fast—like nothing I've ever seen or played on before, or since. They're almost a purple-y blue color—not even green—and cut down crazy short. Like a shaved military private's head—if a green could ever be a shaved head. Mind-blowing fast. Blew mine out the water. Kristi's, too. When you grow up playing mostly as a public course kid, you seldom ever play fast greens, much less this insanely fast.

I remember going back to the main practice green, the one behind the first tee and just back of the 10th. Lots of subtle slopes and elevations, though it's harder to appreciate from outside the ropes. I'm rolling putts, thinking about tomorrow, Thursday, my opening round at the Masters, and it takes not one, not two, but three to realize I have putted off the practice green with all three of my putts.

Putted off the green!

So then I just *drop* the balls onto the green and watch in amazement as they land and trickle off the green so methodically you could read the Titleist logo with each rotation.

I'll never forget watching Fuzzy on number 6, the straightaway par 3 with the elevated green. Banked green, slopes aplenty. Fuzzy has a little six-footer for birdie after a great shot in, the pin back left, but he's above the hole. He taps it like you might a crystal wine glass, to make that resonating ting-ing sound, butterfly with sore feet kind of soft, and I watch in amazement as the ball rolls by the hole a good four feet. (Had he hit it any softer I'm not sure the ball would have moved at all.) Trickling might be the better word. I can read the writing on the ball as it keeps going and going. Not that I wasn't on the defensive with my flat stick already, after putting off the practice green the evening before—three times!—but what I just witnessed sends me into lockdown.

And to think, come Sunday, Tiger will break the tourna-ment scoring record on greens like these. He will flat-out own them. It doesn't surprise me in the least, though, and I find it awe-inspiring. Mind-blowing. Magical stuff. Disney-esque.

Tiger can flip the switch like nobody else.

Mine just got switched off.

I HAVE A BRIEF MOMENT OF GLORY in my first and only Masters, which is prefaced by a rookie mistake. I am 5-over through seven holes—just a brutal start. I'm also nervous as a preacher with no sermon. Can't get it in the hole with both hands and a plunger. I'm on the 8th hole, the par 5 up the hill—the one the caddies call Big Bertha (yes, that's where Ely Callaway got the name from—I'll tell you that story some other time.) I'm hacking it around, with a 30-foot putt for par. This is back when we wore metal spikes on our shoes, and my shoes are thick as thieves with rye grass, like I'm walking on green rye grass biscuits. I finally have a moment to clean them off, as I wait for Fuzzy to hit his pitch shot after two nice shots to pin high. And so I do, pulling a tee out of my pocket to dig the

grass out of my spikes; I'm on the right-hand side of the green.
And that is exactly where the stuff, the massive amount of rye
grass, falls off my shoes.

Onto the fringe, not the green itself. Bad idea, apparently.

A green coat gentleman—a member of Augusta—walks
over and makes it clear that I don't need to do that ever again.
As long as I shall live.

I tell him, "Yes, sir." And he says, "Thank you, *Steve.*"

Hey, he knows my name.

The attention to detail at Augusta is something to behold.

Despite the reprimand—which I get, fair enough—I hole
the 30-footer for par. The patrons in the stands clap in unison
like I just won the thing. And I birdie the 9th, to turn at 40,
also to raucous applause, giving me a little hope for the weekend. Tiger turned at 40, too.

The hope was brief.

It's a cool, crisp morning for my first and only Masters
appearance. Temperature in the mid-40s. The air crisp as ice-
berg lettuce. Everything around me just postcard-perfect beautiful. A memory for the nursing home.

And I will never forget it—as long as I live.

AFTER MISSING THE CUT ON FRIDAY, I head to the rental house,
my Masters experience over. It's a bummer, no doubt. Not that
I expected to win by any stretch (although Tiger obviously did),
but I did think I could make the cut with Kristi on my bag—
make a little noise, maybe win the Low Amateur, get a little
airtime with Jim Nantz in the Butler Cabin.

Turns out no amateur makes the cut that year, so there is
no Low Amateur.

Funny thing is, I have never had as much fun playing

poorly. Sneaking in to the Champions locker room my first night in the Crow's Nest—it's right there at the bottom of those crazy-steep stairs.

Nicklaus has just the one Green Jacket hanging in his locker, by the way. I guess they put the same one on him all six times he won. Don't see that written down in any of the history books.

I had to do it. I had to sneak down there. I think Bobby Jones would approve. At least I hope so.

34

OB-LA-DI, OB-LA-DA

AFTER THE MASTERS, I MAKE SOME DUMB choices.

Actually, I make some of them before. And we probably should swap out the word *some* with the words *a bunch*.

Although I win the Dogwood Invitational, a pretty high-end amateur event, one of the biggest in the country, coming on the heels of finishing second in the Dixie Amateur, the Sunnehanna, and the Northeast in '96, where I bogey the last four holes to lose by a shot, my golf in '97 is not quite great, not quite where I need it to be to reach my goals of playing on the PGA Tour. Winning on the PGA Tour. I have every intention of coming back to the Masters and winning it.

When you get in the limelight a little bit, in my case a lot of bit—for me, anyway—you start listening to what people say, something I never really did before. I only hit the ball right to left. Can't hit a fade to save my life—still can't, to this day. But I wanted to learn how to hit a fade—the greatest golfers of all time hit fades (the names Hogan and Nicklaus come to mind), so I start monkeying with my swing a little bit. When the pin is tucked right, I want to be able to fade it in.

Surely, I can do that, right?

When the pin is tucked right, for me, I have to play off the green to get it close. And if I don't hit that sweeping draw just so, my Titleist ends up in the spinach.

I did it to try to be more of a complete ball striker. To be able to go after a right pin by starting at the middle of the green. The final pin at the '96 US Am is a right pin; the two playoff holes are both right pins; the 34th hole where I tell Tiger to move his mark back—that's a right-side pin.

I often miss greens right when the pin is on the right—especially if I'm trying to make birdie. Of course, there are other things besides my inability to hit a fade when needed that cost me the '96 US Am. But I do think it could have changed the outcome, or at least the way I went out, had I done so properly. *Challenged* might be the better word.

It's the line you teeter across when you're a very good player.

You're just trying to get another tenth of a shot out of your game.

You're just trying to squeeze a little more juice out of the orange. But is the juice worth the squeeze?

It's such a fine line.

ALL OF A SUDDEN, I LOSE WHAT I'M really good at—drawing the ball at will. Suddenly, I can't draw a stickman.

I do manage to win the Dogwood Invitational hitting a fade more often than not, *somehow*—but it's really dumb, what I do. Changing what I am good at, great at, midstream into my dream. I go down a bit of a bad road. Why would I change my swing from a draw to a fade when I was about to play Augusta—a golf course that screams for a draw?

Because I was young and dumb, I guess.

Actually, I don't really know.

My putting stroke is long and flowy, and I decel a lot at Augusta, because the speeds of the greens have me scared not just half, but fully to death. I have to adjust my stroke. Imagine adjusting the pace that defines your walk. Basically, changing your personality. While there, at Augusta, I'm living the yips, and boy, is it some kind of awful. I don't have the money to hire some fancy Butch Harmon-type swing coach. I can't hire the guidance I probably need, to handle all the stuff that's coming at me like a T Rex and me stalled in my Jurassic Park Jeep. I don't have anybody to call on that has been there, has done that.

I become a big ol' mess.

Debilitating.

It's a lot my fault—I was pretty dumb to do some of the things I did. Trying to change my natural swing, the same swing that brought me to the cusp of the greatest finals match in US Amateur history. Who does that?

But when you're grasping for straws, every straw looks like a potential winner. Plastic, paper, metal. You try them all. You reach for them all; even when they slip through your fingers, you keep reaching.

In 1999, my last year as an Amateur, having rallied the troops—I'm holding onto my putter, starting in late '98, with it tucked against my arm (along with some other modifications to make my hands basically immobile, so they can't screw up) à la two-time Masters champion Bernhard Langer—having found myself and my golf swing again (I go back to hitting my best golf swing friend, the sweeping draw), I'm the number-one amateur golfer in the world.

The number-one amateur golfer in the world. How about that?

I win five events that year, which is a bunch in top-shelf amateur/college golf. Two amateur events, three collegiate events, including our home event, The Gator Invitational— with all the big boys in town—as well as The Queens Harbor Invitational in Jacksonville, and the Chris Schenkel in Statesboro, Georgia. Place called Forest Heights. Great track. Huge event. Again, all the big Division 1 schools are there. I remember they had a beer machine next to where they parked the carts. Fifty cents for a cold one. Just drop in a couple quarters and down drops a 16-ounce solo cup and in flows draught beer. Never seen anything like that before. Pretty clever device.

I even win SEC Player of the Year. I feel born again, to tell you the truth. To be the medalist in three out of our four collegiate tournaments we play the spring of my senior year—that's pretty much unheard of. I am on top of the world. Time to turn pro. What else is the number-one ranked amateur in the world supposed to do? Nothing left to prove.

And yet, I am scared to death. *Unsure* might be the better word. What now?

Kristi and I will marry that year, both of us still in college. To marry, while still in college. That's crazy, I know. But I love her, and love knows no boundaries. Perhaps you've been there, too. It's not a bad place to be.

I miss out on Q school in '99; I do, however, make it to the finals of Q school in December of 2000, but once again I am matches with no cigar to light. I am fortunate enough to be gifted five sponsor exemptions in 2000, though I do very little with them.

Kristi is still on my bag. And I am now what they call conditional on the PGA Tour, playing on the Nationwide Tour, now called the Korn Ferry. I get opportunities to play on the PGA Tour, but they are all on call. I never know if I'm going to get to play until literally the moment before the whistle blows.

Conditional.

How am I going to make money to support my family?

Could I be any more lost?

I end up caddying at Seminole Golf Club, Ben Hogan's favorite course, and it's easy to see why. The Wee Iceman felt that if you could play well at Seminole, you could play well anywhere. I caddy there for a few winters as I'm trying to make it on Tour. In the year 2000, I get a few sponsor invites for some Tour events, which I appreciate more than I can say, but I don't do well. Actually, I don't make any cuts.

I'm just trying to make ends meet, which at the time felt like trying to turn kitchen string into bungee cord.

It's really weird when you turn pro. The game of golf changes from something you once did for fun to something you have to do. To work, to survive. You're married, you have to support your family. You need to make a few bucks. Make that a lot of bucks. I don't do a really good job about that.

Tough row to hoe.

I end up hoeing that tough row up in Canada, on their professional Tour. Which is a good one, by the way. And the Canadians are as nice a folk as you would ever want to meet. But I don't make a whole lot of money up in the Great White North, either. I make some, sure, but not a lot.

Two thousand five is my last year of playing professionally. I probably put too much pressure on myself, but it's time for me to go, and I know it. I'm sitting in my car in the parking lot of PGA National Golf Club. Defeated. I tie up my self-worth with my golf.

I've never told this story to anyone before, but now that I'm literally an open book, why hold anything back?

It's 2005, and I'm finishing up my degree at Florida Atlantic University in Boca Raton. I have ten classes on the table. Knock 'em out, Steve ol' boy, and your diploma awaits. But, well, damn. I'm such a comprehensive mess right now, it's all I can do to sign my scorecard, much less pass Calculus II.

Can we rewind for a second? If you don't you mind?

It's late September of 2004—and I'm coming off a pretty decent season on the Canadian Tour, finishing fourth over-all on the money list, almost winning in Calgary in a playoff. Another almost, but an almost just the same. Earlier in the year, I've taken a number of lessons from Bob Toski, unquestionably one the greatest golf instructors of all time. (This will later segue me into my third career in life—teaching the game of golf. Bob teaches me *so* much about the golf swing, during a time when I am trying desperately to fix my own.)

I'm feeling pretty good about my game, about my life; except, well, I'm not. I'm over the doldrums of 2003, but I'm not really loving the travel, the hotel life, and I'm not advancing in my golf game the way I want to, need to. I'm simply not getting as much out of the game as I want.

I can see the end of the road in the headlights, and as much as I want to turn those headlights off, I turn on the bright lights instead. I'm thinking I want to do something else with my life. Pretty much anything but this.

Bob Ford, who I was incredibly fortunate to play two rounds of the US Open with back in '96, well, we had stayed in touch. I end up playing in a Pro Am at Oakmont and stay in Bob's house, which is maybe fifty yards off the 18th green. Bob was kind enough to host me—and I was very much appreciative of his unconditional friendship. I get to spend a lot of time with Bob in the evenings—lots of time to chat and ponder life.

Bob lays out the land of what being a club pro would be about, and I am mightily intrigued, hanging on his every word the way I once hung on to Ray's words back on that driving range in Florida. I can hear his voice loud and clear: "Chase your hands to your hips, Steve."

Bob tells me how long it will likely take me to climb up the ranks of the head pro world. It's a touch discouraging, I won't lie—putting one thing aside, and starting anew, but I'm ready.

It's time to move on.

One thing that sticks out in my memory of that last night of talking with Bob—sticks out like the first time you see the flying monkeys from the *Wizard of Oz* and you are only four years old and you pee your pants when you see them come down from out of nowhere and swoop up poor little Toto—is when Bob says to me, "Steve, I wouldn't hire you to come work for me if you didn't have a degree. I don't care how impressive your pedigree is."

I don't have a degree.

This gets the hamsters rolling in my head.

Everybody wants to work for Bob Ford. He is *the* golden ticket into the golf business. Whether you work at Oakmont, Pine Valley, or you name it. Bob is the head pro down at Seminole, if that tells you anything—still is to this day.

I have a talk with Kristi soon after my time with Bob, and

him telling me the honest truth about no degree, no hire. I have a whole year to finish up. I can do this.

Ten classes stand between me and that cap and gown.

Now, I'm living down in South Florida, and I head over to Florida Atlantic University and enroll in the communications program. FAU is where I finally get my degree. I take five classes in the spring of 2005, and in the summer of that same year I play the Golden Bear Tour, which is pretty much organized legal gambling, but well structured and you play great tracks. I still have the itch to play competitive golf, and it is scratching me like a briar patch. I fare decently in my endeavors out there, make a little money back, but I don't fare too well when it is all said and done. The wolf is still at the door.

It's toward the end of the season on The Golden Bear Tour, and I will never forget this, as long as I walk this Earth.

It's the first round of the tournament, and I'm starting on the back 9 of the PGA National. I'm playing okay—just very average. We make the turn, and I make a couple pars on one and two. Number three, my 12th of the day, is a reachable par 5. And the pin is on the right-hand side.

My old nemesis.

We are taking carts, mind you. I don't have Kristi on my bag.

I'm riding with an Aussie named Aron Price, who lives in Jacksonville. Fellow Floridian. I think he still plays professionally—not sure where, exactly.

I hit driver off the tee. Stripe a pretty decent one. Have maybe 255 to the flagstick. A perfect cut driver off the deck, one of my favorite shots to hit, and I hit it pretty sweet, but I overcut it *just* a touch and it ends up in the greenside bunker. It's an easy up and down; the ball sitting up and looking pretty.

An up and down you'll make nine times out of ten—at least on this level.

I dig my heels in and hit a mediocre shot, and then I miss the putt for birdie.

I make par.

I am livid. This is not the way it's supposed to go. I can't *not* make birdie on this hole, one of the easiest on the course.

I walk over to the golf cart—where my bag is strapped in like a deer on the hood of a crappy-ass pickup, the way it looks to me right now—and I get in the cart, and the windshield is like, well, it has the plastic connectors that secure it to the frame. One of the connectors was exposed, but I don't see it.

The connectors are rubber, but they are a really *hard* rubber. Like concrete can be hard. The reason I say this is I took my fist, and I punched the cart as hard as I could.

I'm not proud of that. But I don't regret it, because that jackass move—for which I am very sorry for as to how it came about—actually changed my life.

Forever.

After my Mike Tyson imitation, the middle finger of my right hand splits open, like something out of the movies. Holy Moly. Blood spurting from the wound, and now I'm bleeding like a stuck pig. I can't grip the club; it hurts so bad. I try, but as I do, the grip becomes covered in blood and it's slick as can be, and blood is going everywhere. Drips off the grip, onto my pants, my shirt, the grass. I'm standing there looking like something out of a B-grade horror movie. But I did it to myself. If there were a full-length mirror to look into, I would be hanging my head like fat over a belt buckle.

I say to my group, "Guys, I'm done." I apologize for being

so, but I really was truly done. Done with the playing of the game of golf forever. I was just that damn done.

I take my clubs off the cart—how funny that I would take my clubs off the cart even though I was, in my mind at the time, never going to swing them again. To hell with it—why not just leave them there—and I start walking, golf bag slung over my shoulder, blood still dripping all over the place, clubs clanging in my golf bag with each heavy-hearted step I take.

My golf bag.

Okay, you know I am sentimental. It's okay to laugh at the picture I've just painted. A Bob Ross it is not. No pretty little trees are hanging around here.

YOUR GOLF BAG IS AKIN TO YOUR CAR, your old-school wheels as you travel down the highways of life, be it a Mazda RX7 when you meet the love of your life at the local mall and you think you are one cool cat, or a beat-to-hell silver Honda Accord, when you roll down Magnolia Lane in the middle of the night scared shitless, and the next morning they tell you to move that piece of junk somewhere else. Anywhere but here, rookie.

She's your girl; your golf bag is your girl. She needs to be on your shoulder, or your caddy's shoulder, in a professional event, not strapped to the back of some golf cart that doesn't know you from Adam.

My girl and her contents have been so good to me over the years. At this moment, I'm not so sure how good I have been to her. At least not right now. What a mess I am making right now, but I can't stop until the mess has been fully made.

I know it's over for me, the dream of playing golf professionally, for a living.

My heart is broken, and I wonder if I've broken hers, too.

So with my bag on my shoulder as I traipse up the hill, a couple-holes-walk back to the clubhouse, I see a building in the distance. I don't think too much of it, as I'm saying good-bye to the life I always dreamed of having in the golf world.

Life has a wicked sense of humor. It hurts and it heals—sometimes both at the same time.

Turns out the building is the Golf Digest Golf School, ironically—or maybe not—the teaching school Bob Toski founded. It's right there, at PGA National. In fact, I have a friend who works there.

I drive right over. Immediately. I get in my car and head right over, my rejected clubs in the trunk. It is truly time for a change. As Clint Eastwood said in the classic movie *Magnum Force*, "A man has got to know his limitations." I now know mine. I'm just not cut out for the PGA Tour as a player.

I inquire about a job, at Bob Toski's place across the street, and it's one I soon get.

I become a teacher. As Kristi likes to say, Toski gave me the vocabulary and the understanding to explain to my students why the golf ball does what it does as it takes off into the great wide-open once it leaves your clubface.

She's right.

Man, do I love to teach. It gives me great satisfaction to put a smile on someone's face knowing I gave them the knowledge they didn't have the hour before we met. Passing on my knowledge of the game—helping people get better because of the experiences that I've had, or *through* the experiences I've had—is incredibly rewarding. Maybe somebody will have more talent than I have, more drive, more patience and all of that, and I can teach them something that I've learned, maybe a lot of somethings, that helps them go on to win pro tournaments, maybe even majors.

Or just win any tournament at all.

The majority of golfers who actually play the game of golf have very little idea just how hard it is to win a tournament. So many stars have to align, so many pieces have to fall in place regardless the puzzle, be it junior golf, college golf, amateur circuit, the minitours, the PGA Tour, the Senior Tour, the local club championship.

In teaching, there is such a different satisfaction from in playing. Better, at least to me. It goes back to the connection I spoke of earlier. You have that beautiful connection between you and your student, or you and the member of your club. But when you are a touring pro, and by that, I mean one who's out there playing for a living where every stroke means a dollar— in most cases thousands of dollars—it's just so cutthroat out there. You're just trying to beat one another's brains in. The human connection is the furthest thing from your mind.

Where is the fun in that?

I END UP EARNING MY WAY INTO the PGA of America, which changes everything.

In 2007, I become a Class A PGA professional, which means you are a rock star, but also one of thousands of said rock stars looking for a job at a golf club, location be damned. You will move to the North Pole and moonlight for Santa if it means an opportunity.

My first head pro job is in 2009, in New Jersey, at The Ridge at Back Brook. I'm there for three years. That's almost 1,000 days of 24–7. You show up at sunrise and you head home when the sun is just about to come up again—or at least that's often how it feels—to me, anyway. Then I spend six years at the Paramount Country Club in the MET section in New York.

Kristi and I go on to have kids.

Oh, man.

Having kids will change your life like air conditioning changed the courtroom, microwaves changed the kitchen. And it will change your heart in ways unimaginable. Magical, both of our kiddos. J.C., who is now twelve, and our daughter, Kaylie, who is now ten, are the apples of my eye.

Boy, time flies fast.

These days, I run tournaments, instead of playing in them, although every now and again I get to play in a few, like the Wells Fargo, the Wyndham Championship, the RBC Heritage, top-notch PGA Tour events all. I raise my kids with my heart on my sleeve and love my wonderful wife with every ounce of my being. What can I say? I love them all like crazy.

I'm also head pro for The Outpost Club, and the founder of the Silver Club Golfing Society. I do a little podcasting, teach some here and there—I'm currently Director of Instruction for *Golfweek Magazine*. Every now and again, I'll put a peg in the ground and see if I've still got it—or if I gotta *go* and find it. I'm headed to the North Carolina Open as we speak, with my shoelaces untied.

We shall see.

35

REFLECTION

THERE IS A SAYING THAT REALLY STICKS with me. It came into my life seven years ago when I got lost. One of the things Kristi and I really talked about, as I got my lost game back. Man, I was lost for so long.

Every player has a golfing DNA. For me, it's my draw. And the ability to make key putts when I have to make them. Be a competitive, fiery player. A grinder. *Will* the ball into the hole.

Never give up. Grind like the grist in the mill.

It has served me well over the years. It will serve you well, too. If there was ever any advice I could give to you that would stick, it would be this.

Something happened in there, in the vacuum of getting lost—I got away from that; something got lost in the translation. I got lost in the translation, as well. Trying to hit a fade, messing with my putting grip. Trying to get better for whatever reason, for all the wrong reasons.

Kristi gives me this maxim, and it's a perfect saying: "Protect your fortress, Steve."

All the best golfers have this fortress. Walls built up around them. Built up around their castle, be it made of stone or wood or even straw. The people who succeed are the ones who maintain the integrity of those walls. The ones who don't, they have a tougher time—the ones who let others permeate those walls have a tougher time, too. And by that I mean stay true to you; be the golfer you were born to be, hit that plastic ball with your plastic club through your galley kitchen, give it a rip and let the chips fall where they may.

That's from Kristi. I failed her, but later in life I came back to her wisdom. What has really helped me in my golf game over the last seven years is sticking to that mindset. I am a great player. I know I can play this game. God has given me that gift. That is also from Michael Breed, former Augusta assistant pro and now one of the top golf instructors in the world, who woke me back up when I was knee-deep in the abyss and said, "Play golf the way you were born onto this Earth to play, Steve. Play that sweeping draw!"

But there *is* a fortress you have to protect. That you absolutely must protect. Pull the drawbridge over the moat so they can't cross over. You have a certain amount of skills that you have to put that amount of trust in. Know what you are good at and be stubborn about it.

Not just have to, you must. Trust in you.

So, to all of you out there: protect your fortress. Take it from me. I know firsthand what happens when you don't.

36

DREAM SEQUENCE, OF REAL LIFE, THAT NEVER ACTUALLY HAPPENED

I'M TWO UP WITH THREE TO GO. I hit my bunker shot out there, hole my putt for par. I am pumped beyond words, jazzed as Preservation Hall. I'm not even looking back at Tiger, not even looking in that direction. Looking instead at Kristi.

I haven't looked in Tiger's direction all day. Why would I look there now?

I don't want to get caught up in what he is doing.

I make my putt for par, but I'm not even looking back at Tiger. I'm walking to the 17th tee, and the gallery is in the way. But my footsteps are slow. Like I can't really see exactly what's going on. Like it's foggy, or something. But I hear the crowd gasp. And the gasp is not what I think it is. I think: He's hit the putt and missed the putt. Didn't make his birdie.

Then, someone in the crowd yells, "Hey, Steve, you won!" From someone who was looking.

I wasn't looking.

And I think to myself, *What are you talking about?*

The USGA Rules officials are there in an instant, looking forlorn, a bit confused, and I don't understand. I'm ready to go to the next tee. Keep this match rolling.

I'm waiting, and listening for Tiger's putt to go in, but I hear this gasp from the crowd. But the gasp is not what I think it is. It's not the fact Tiger's missed the putt. It's something else entirely. It's like I'm out of body.

The Rules official comes over.

Tiger played from the wrong spot.

In a way, I can see him set up, over the top of the gallery, from the wrong spot, but I'm too far away to say anything. I get a better look at what's going on, and I see Tiger's head sunk down in his hands. The Rules official, right there. Talking to Tiger. A hand on his shoulder. It's so out of body, like I'm not even there, yet I am.

"Hey, you won! Steve, you just won the US Amateur!"

The trophy is coming over, silver and shiny with the sunlight bouncing off the gleaming metal to the point where I have to squint my eyes, and I'm the winner.

The winner.

Of the 1996 US Amateur. Against the exponentially great Tiger Woods.

HAD I WALKED TO THE LEFT, after picking my ball out of the hole when I made my par putt, and not walked to the right, which I could just have easily done, that is exactly what would have happened.

And that is what wakes me up from my dream.

But that is no way to win the United States Amateur. At least I think so. I hope you do, too. Best loss ever.

Best loss *ever.*

But yeah, it hurts like a weird sadness. How could it not? To be so proud of yourself, and heartbroken at the same time. I knew my life would never be the same. Tiger's, either.

You know, it's funny, looking back on it some 25 years later as I am about to put down my pen from this year-and-a-half journey of writing this book. My life turned out better than I could have ever imagined. So did Tiger's.

I guess it was meant to be.

But isn't all of this meant to be?

37

AN OPEN LETTER TO TIGER

ONE FINAL THOUGHT FROM ME

Dear tiger,

I have to first say how incredibly difficult it was to see your horrific car accident in Los Angeles yesterday. I know that you were on the mend from your recent back surgery and looking forward to competing in this year's Masters as well as other majors. I am very sorry that this will undeniably set you back regarding all of your hopes, and I know I'm not alone when I say my main wish now is for you to return to good health and simply be there for your family, whatever that looks like. Major championships or not.

Speaking of family, watching you recently in the PNC Championship with your son, Charlie, it looks like the apple didn't fall far from the tree, with your son taking up the game and starting to win already. I'm sure your daughter has your competitive spirit, too. My 12-year-old son and 10-year-old daughter enjoy the game but don't play it too seriously, but maybe one day. The only thing my wife, Kristi, and I care about is that they understand all the values the game offers.

I know we haven't connected in a long time since I sent you that picture from our match to sign for me back in 2009, which you did, and many thanks for that; but I framed that picture, and it now proudly hangs in my home office and reminds me every day of the great—I like to call it epic—match that we had way back in 1996. It was more than a great match; it was a surreal moment in time and an atmosphere that I have never encountered before, or since. I imagine in many ways you feel the same, but as many amazing victories as you have had over the years, I could understand if you viewed our match as just another blip on the timeline, but I hope you don't.

Looking back, I imagine you feel what I feel.

Can you believe it's been 25 years since that match? Our career paths both converged and diverged about as quickly as they could with me never having made it full-time on the PGA Tour and you jumping into the deep end of stardom straight-away. I have been a PGA Professional now going on fifteen years and love helping people improve their game, running tournaments for my club members, and yes, I still compete and have played in a few Tour events in the Carolinas PGA Section in the last few years. I never really had the distance to compete back then, and I sure don't have the distance now (even though I can still carry it 270), so I'm glad I made the career-path decision I did at the point that I did. I also do some golf broadcasting, having worked for FOX at their USGA events (until NBC took them over) and a few other entities, like PGA Tour Live. It's a lot of fun.

Just like you, I still love so many aspects of the game.

Funny sidebar story . . . you didn't realize this at the time, but during the 2018 US Open at Shinnecock, I was covering the 11th hole in a featured-hole coverage when you played it and then came up to the 12th tee where I was standing (as that was a nice perch to see the play on the 11th and 12th tees). I'm standing just back and right of the teeing ground, and your group came up and hit their shots. After your tee shot that you pull-hooked left into the tall fescue, you came back toward where I was standing, but we never locked eyes. You were literally three feet away, and I could hear you muttering something in frustration. You were so close I could have tapped you on the shoulder. I almost laughed and said something like, "Why didn't you do that sh#!t against me?"

It was funny to me because it was really the closest, physically, I've been to you since we saw each other at a few Tour events in the early 2000s (I think it was the parking lot at Pebble Beach where we crossed paths and exchanged a few pleasantries). In fact, I have always wanted to sit down and chat with you about our epic match and the impact it had on both of us. Maybe someday we will.

I would like that.

There were so many epic moments of that August 25th day back in '96 that are burned into both of our memories, and I think at some point sooner rather than later it would be fun to meet up and reminisce about your last day as an amateur golfer. Our names will be inexorably linked from that one day of golf that changed our lives forever. I know it was your crowning achievement in golf, something that will never be duplicated in our lifetimes or many lifetimes to come. Yet, in so many ways and with all that transpired that fateful day, it was my crowning achievement, as well.

I have thought of so many "what-if" scenarios over the

years. What would've really happened if I didn't remind you to move your mark back on the 34th hole? How would we both have gone on from there, with me winning the Havemeyer Trophy and you finishing second? Would you have turned pro the next day? Would Nike have given you a forty-million-dollar contract? Would you have gone on to change the way the world views the game of golf the following spring in Augusta, winning by 12 shots and blowing away the field if you didn't gain all the confidence you did from miraculously coming back from the dead to beat me and subsequently winning two Tour events that fall?

How would your career path have been different (or would it have?)?

How would mine have been changed?

Some answers in life we will never know, and at the same time, we aren't supposed to know all of them. I believe that life always turns out the way it's supposed to, and you and I were meant to face each other that fateful day. Destiny plays a defining role in all our lives, and I was supposed to be your opponent that day and give you one of the toughest matches, if not the toughest match, you've ever had. I was supposed to be the tough adversary that you had to face one last time before you set sail in the professional ranks. I was supposed to be there on the 34th hole to essentially become your guiding light to remind you not to make an error of grave proportion, to give a cool nod to the great golf announcer Ben Wright. Why the golf gods chose me, we'll never know.

On the one hand, I helped you win, but on the other hand, you helped me win, too. It's a moment to this day I would never have done any differently, for myself, for you, and for the game that we both love. You were destined to do the things you did on the golf course to change the game forever, and I was destined to play the role that I played, and continue to play, in golf. Just so you know, I've pulled for you all along the way to achieve what you have, and to break all the records in golf that you have, and even though you've been through hell and back recently, I know you're not done being the Tiger Woods that everyone knows you can be. But if for some reason you don't play another competitive shot again, I will forever remember with great pride our moment creating history at Pumpkin Ridge.

Take care.

Sincerely,
Steve

AFTERWORD: THE RETURN TO PUMPKIN RIDGE: ONE CADDY'S REFLECTIONS OF THE 1996 US AMATEUR CHAMPIONSHIP 25 YEARS HENCE

BY KRISTI HOMMEL SCOTT

THE TERMINATOR.

Us against the World.

I'm diving deeper into my catalog of memories, one last time, as 25 years have allowed these memories time to marinate, just a bit.

Maybe a *lot* a bit.

When I close my eyes, there are always two vivid memories that pop to the surface like a Coca-Cola red bobber when the fish gets away.

Number one thought is actually just before the first hole, before that finals match is played. The air is cool and thick with mist, in this Portland, Oregon, morning. I'm standing on the practice putting green, watching through the fog, as the groggy sun starts to wake up. I'm soaking in this eerie, ominous energy as I look around back at the clubhouse. It's quiet and calm as I look to Steve and return his putts over and over to him while he warms up.

Just rolling them back to him along the ground. So he can see the breaks I see.

Maybe it's because we've entered into our bubble for the day; I'm not paying any attention to the loyal patrons to the game, who are arriving by the hundreds—the thousands, actually.

The dew is thick on the grass, rolling up onto my socks as we stroll up to the first tee nice and early to meet the officials, Tiger, and his caddy. I put the bag down near the tee markers on the right and stare down the first fairway, and I have to catch my breath. I can't even count how many spectators just magically showed up lining the fairway.

Huh? This isn't a PGA Tour event. Yet, how cool is this?

There's a very serious vibe on the first tee, and I get a sense the teeing ground is morphing into a boxing ring; we retreat to our corner, getting ready for the announcer to get the show started. What a duel this is in store; and as I look at my honey for that last little good luck (I know you're going to kick butt, honey) stare, we exchange little smirks to each other knowing, without knowing, this is going to be one hell of a day.

Boy, we had no idea.

Number two thought/memory: I'm instantly in the back-seat of that beige rental car Chrysler sedan, peering out the window with a bittersweet smile staring back at that Pumpkin

Ridge entrance sign one last time, my body slowly returning to Earth as my aching feet are like an anchor back to reality. Driving away from a moment in time that burns so vividly in my mind and, as I've come to realize, in the minds of many thousands, even millions that day.

A moment in golf history, but this time, I have the benefit of the rearview mirror mindset.

And as I sit there, in that Chrysler backseat headed east, I can feel the release of the day, of every shot, of every putt, of every cheer, of every defeat, of every fist pump, of every breath of hope just slowly dissolve into a place waiting for me to revisit again.

WHAT WE KNEW THEN WAS TIGER WAS A phenom in what he could accomplish, and how damn far he could hit the ball. I learned that he worked with a sports psychologist. Interesting concept, especially at that time, when having specialists train and travel with you was a brand-new concept. What did they do, together, I had wondered? What did they talk about? What questions were asked on that driving range between the first and second 18s of our epic match?

Plus, Tiger has a swing coach who *travels* with him.

The year is 1996.

Unheard of, this.

What amateur in the world has a swing coach, and in this case one who travels with him? What is that like? What other professionals does Tiger need to travel with him? *Huh—this Tiger guy must need a lot of help* was also a thought that ran through my mind at the time.

But as time went on, to learn of this team of world-class professionals that travels with him, and agents that hung on his dad Earl's every last word, and the depth of training Tiger endured starting from, well, could he even walk yet when it all started?

Tiger was essentially the terminator, from the second movie, *Terminator 2, Judgment Day*, but not the good terminator. Tiger was that liquid one in that second eighteen holes of our finals match. No matter what you shoot at it, or how you tried to kill it, it just kept coming back, respawning.

With no lava in sight for us to save the day.

Terminator—yes, definitely an accurate account.

I HAD CADDIED FOR STEVE IN QUITE A FEW pretty huge amateur events leading up to this US Am, including the US Open (wow!!) just a few months prior to this historic day, this grueling week. And the one common thread among all competitors we played with prior to Tiger was that they were still human.

Human.

There was always some point during a round where there would be a form of conversation, a mutual admiration for good shots. Maybe not said after every single shot, but honestly, that is one of the many cool things about golf. You acknowledge when a player has performed a great shot—that is the gentleman/gentlewoman part, or at least the classy part, of this crazy game.

Like no other game in the world.

I coach girls' golf in this present day, and that's the one thing I love most about our matches and practices—the encouragement and acknowledgment of teammates and opponents alike. In men's golf, which, ironically, I found myself involved in at the top levels thanks to Steve, well, it groomed me into learning that such acknowledgments are as natural as breathing.

When a golfer sticks their approach shot inside three feet, you acknowledge it. Well done, great shot. And when the circumstances reflect very tough conditions to pull off such a great shot, there is even more emphasis. I think I appreciated that most when caddying for Steve. To see the contrast in how the guys play vs. the girls.

Your game did the talking, and when your game made a strong point, you acknowledge it.

That's what golf instilled in me. This is where class and sport are blended together, and the higher the stakes, the more a person's character is revealed.

I'm far from perfect as a player, but I definitely appreciate that golf teaches you to be the best version of yourself, if you're paying attention to the lessons.

Even then, during intense, competitive rounds with Steve and with me on the bag, there was always a point in the day where you'd have to wait on a slow group, or something—there was almost always some light conversation to just blow off some steam.

So, where are you from? Oh cool, so you are a Gators fan.

What's your favorite color?

Kidding, that last question would never come up.

Either Steve initiated or it came from a fellow golfer in the group. That sort of behavior was light years away from the Finals Match with Tiger. The only human being among Tiger's group was his caddy—which I appreciated, as we would exchange the flag from hole to hole as caddies do. You grab it on one, I'll grab it on two, or wherever, depending on who is away or who holes out first. But it was a cordial energy—on par for what seemed normal to me.

NOPE, TIGER WAS THE INVINCIBLE—UNLESS SWIMMING in lava—Terminator.

Aside from the quick handshake and introduction on the first tee, there would be silence between the two, Steve and Tiger—or at least one-way silence. "Nice shot, Tiger," Steve would say; yeah, second nature to us, but a big ask coming from the other direction.

A big ask that was never answered.

But that's okay, Steve didn't need Tiger's approval. Steve was not a machine. He was a whole bunch of swagger, sure, with his own invincibility and belief in himself. Steve was at the peak of his game. And it wasn't because he was groomed by top instructors, or trainers, or sports psychologists, or frankly any fancy training whatsoever.

There was Ray telling him to hit the telephone pole out in the distance off a rubber mat with low-flight golf balls. Turn those golf balls just so, Steve, so the red striped paint doesn't get on your clubs. There were his dad's words of encouragement, and then there is the kindness of Goose. And that was so many years ago.

Not saying those are bad things; in fact, they are quite beautiful.

So, on that postcard-perfect August summer day, there were no paid professionals in Steve's camp. Just his girlfriend, aunt, and uncle, and without the latter two, I, the girlfriend, wasn't even supposed to be there.

Such a far cry from how Tiger grew up. A canyon. The Grand one. North rim and South rim combined. How many moments of instruction was Steve fortunate enough to have?

A handful, with a few fingers missing.

Yet, those rudimentary lessons were priceless, and yet Steve paid nothing. Never was charged a nickel—can you believe that? Huge heart for this magical game was always all around him. I wish I could have met his teacher, Ray.

Through Steve, I think maybe I have.

STEVE WAS ALL FEEL, LIKE THE WAY YOU might reach out and grab a ripe peach off a tree. Technicalities were far from his vocabulary, as distant as dandelions in a March wind.

Maybe Steve couldn't explain the ball flight laws or causes or effects of all of the forces of the golf swing; but he didn't have to. If he wanted his ball to go somewhere, he willed it there. It might be a gorgeous shot, or it might be a scrappy shot—but make no mistake, it was going.

The benefit of being with Steve all the time our senior year of high school, which meant we hung out on the golf course pretty much every day, is that I learned so much about the game, but mostly how *he* played it. I learned his funny little quirks (waggles, waddles, and all) that made his game tick and dived farther into his mind than any sports psychologist could ever dream of diving.

And this is how I understood not to worry should his tee shot, or approach shot, not be perfectly down the middle. I actually think his game relaxed when he was behind some trees or in a tough position; this is when he performed miracles. Though perhaps I should call them something else, as he pulled them off time and time again. I got so accustomed to seeing Steve pull off these phenomenal shots that I was more surprised at the times he didn't pull them off than the times when he did.

Steve would see shots like painters see paintings on a blank canvas and feel shots the way musicians feel music in their fingertips without looking at the keys.

Steve would will that ball to do what his mind and body saw fit.

Could not tell a soul how he did what he did, he just did it. As second nature as breathing. It was never about perfect golf for Steve.

You can't teach what Steve has.

Steve becomes the game. He is the course. He is the grain, the wind, the hills all the while he is the ball and how it must fly and roll to get to its final destination. The swing is just energy—the push and pull of forces working together to meet in the perfect moment to create the magic of a great golf shot. Steve plays the way the game was intended to be played. He stands on the tee and unknowingly has an architect's mind, understands the journey the ball must make to triumph each hole. He takes in Mother Nature and course preparation and how they influence each other to change each shot, each hole from day to day, moment to moment. Steve is in the present, taking in the past, and prepping for the future as he steps on to the tee and absorbs that realm as far as the eye can see.

No one taught him this. He was born with it. Like you might be born with a singing voice, an artist's hand, a surgeon's touch.

Steve could imitate legendary swings on cue. My favorite impression was Nick Price. He nailed that one—never saw such a fast swing, and boy he got a kick out of impersonating it. Even up to the waggles. And this would come in handy for me as a caddy one day. Knowing how Steve loves to impersonate his favorite golfers and knowing that nine times out of ten he'd stripe the ball and just stick it to about two feet or less to the hole when he did so.

THE VERY FIRST TIME I CADDIED FOR STEVE was in the '95 US Amateur Qualifier, in the pouring rain, mind you. Horrible rain—cats and dogs and all their friends. We had to go back in it was raining so hard, and I remember them trying to shuttle my family back to the clubhouse with my grandparents barely hanging onto the cart and us in another.

My family loved to watch Steve play—they came out to watch any chance they could.

There came a point during that qualifier when Steve's game was turning south, his energy getting more frustrated, but it was a pressing energy. I had no idea what swing adjustment he needed, but he needed something. His shots were off, but not a consistent off. I knew this was in his head; he was just doing great before, what the heck? No more cruise control for me. And then it hit me, in the middle of the fairway on a par 4, maybe the 12th hole of the round, and I turn to Steve and say, "Hit this shot like Nick Price would." He looked at me kinda funny at first but then bought into it. Took a couple Nick Price practice swings, and I told him, "That's "it! and right before my eyes, he turned into the Nick Price I knew he would be and *bam*, stuck it about a foot.

Made the putt, back in the game.

Steve went on to win that qualifier and later would put the golf world on notice in Rhode Island. That's when he told me straight-faced that I could carry his bag whenever I wanted.

That was the first time I knew how much he trusted me.

It's one thing to have your girlfriend carry your bag for 18 holes. Even that is something many guys wouldn't be comfortable with. But it's a whole new level to give your trust to her and be open to what she says. And then actually *act* on it. It was effortless on both of our parts. Somehow, I knew when to chime in, when to sit back and let him go, and what to say. Steve is the number-one junior golfer in our state of Florida at the time, and he's taking advice from me.

Me?

Funny enough, at that time, I didn't even think of it that way. I was an equal. Never occurred to me I wasn't. And, I guess, Steve agreed. I had only been playing golf for four years, with most of my experience in local events. But perhaps he respected my game enough to know that when you challenge me to a closest-to-the-pin contest, chances are you're going to lose.

Funny how he would wait for a stretch of bad holes from me, but the mere mention of a closest-to-the-pin contest against him, I was game. I think he had learned my game enough to know that's all I needed to get back *in* the game.

Keeping it simple.

Once match play began that week, Steve and I had a formula. It was simple, and we followed it unconditionally. Pick targets off the tee and I remind Steve to finish at the target. Ball flew much straighter this way, that simple reminder to where that ball is going. Little did we know that focusing on targets, especially approach shots, especially on layups, helps a golfer get so much more out of the process of the shot.

If you are an athlete, it's easier to react to something than not. Get your mind involved with where you want to be vs all the millions of thoughts that can haunt you in those precious seconds before starting your backswing.

Man, we had good instincts.

We were in the present, as many sports psychologists will preach, for every shot.

Not that we knew how to do this, we just did.

You've heard of the "zone" and playing in the "zone." That is what it was. Ignorance is bliss and can be helpful to get into that zone. Ignorance of outside factors, of swing thoughts, of pressure.

There was not time for those thoughts.

THE NIGHT BEFORE THE MATCH, STEVE MADE a point to tell me what my job was. Didn't really do this with any other opponent. This was specific to his match against Tiger—do not let Steve deviate from his game. Do not let Steve force his game to do things it simply couldn't do. Play shots he hadn't played all week from off the tee. Tiger wasn't going to change him.

I found this strange—why would this even happen?

Why would Steve all of a sudden hit dumb shots?

Because Tiger's game is an anomaly; it was supreme, and only Tiger could do it.

Those who play against Tiger (apparently) thought they can hit the same shots, use the same clubs, and in doing so fall into the abyss of doom because they would undoubtedly fail at even the attempt to play like Tiger.

Tiger hit the ball farther than humans could hit the ball— and keep it on line. And as I would soon find out, just the sound of impact of Tiger's shots was not like anything I've ever heard.

What the heck kind of clubs is he playing with?

No, it's not his clubs.

It's the swing speed he uses—like a shotgun blast every time he hits the ball. That was unnerving, but interesting. Absolutely do *not* watch his swing, or at least Steve wouldn't. I couldn't help it. Blinders on the whole time for when it could affect his game.

Got it.

The thing is, I don't pay attention to Steve's opponents—don't care about their game. The only one who matters is always Steve. But he needed to express this to be crystal clear. If there was one thing he was committed to, it was to stay true to his own game to the end.

Why wouldn't he? He was steamrolling everyone anyway.

Tiger had to beat Steve, not the other way around, in my book.

AND SO, I FOUND MYSELF LISTENING FOR HIS SWING. I didn't watch Tiger, either. The call of the Sirens wasn't going to pull us into any trance.

Nope. This fortress was ready for battle.

Many wonder if I helped club Steve or read putts. Steve has always liked being in control. If there is one thing he can control, it's his game. And so that's it. I wasn't going to tell him what to do; he knew what to do. He owns every shot. I am there as reassurance, reinforcer, guard rails. Emotions can affect performance in good ways and bad. So, when I detect energy shifting, I do my best to intervene and help shift it back.

Steve is full of energy, intensity—you can see it after every swing. His stare was as potent as Tiger's when holding his finish.

I think that is what's so equal about the both of them. Their determination and unstoppable will was setting the stage for epic performances from each, respectively.

How often did Steve depend on me? I knew how far he hit his clubs. His driver, woods, irons. I read putts in case he needed confirmation; wind direction was always noted. We had our game plan, but so much of what happened that day was autopilot for Steve.

My job that day was not so much on the technical side—
Steve owned that. Mine was to keep emotions in check.

THE LAST 9 HOLES OF THAT FATEFUL DAY is where that would
come into play the most, though the first 18 of the day would
be in stark contrast. I was geared up and ready for this Tyrant
and Tiger-ish golfer, but not a hint of such was visible from
where I stood.

It was on the 6th green where Tiger missed another short
putt, and I turned to Steve in bewilderment—this wasn't even
a contest right now. I gave a big pat on Steve's back, and we just
kept doin' our thing. Big smiles to Steve, who was in the driver's seat, but this was a long day ahead. Pace ourselves. Take
nothing for granted, but at the same time be grateful and tuck
away the successes as they come: may need to reach down to get
their inspiration at some point, but only when needed.

It was on the 8th hole when it dawned on me that Tiger
wasn't much into talking or acknowledging good shots from
Steve.

As in not a *single one.*

The eighth at Pumpkin Ridge is a tough and tricky green
and the approach is key, and though after Tiger hit, I'm pretty
sure we said "shot" (which you know, sometimes you just say
"shot" when you mean good shot—for whatever reason, too
hard to get that other word out I suppose), I remember chatting
with Steve about whether he heard Tiger say that back.

Nope.

Huh. Okay. Fine. We are playing *that* way, are we? I see
how it is.

Tell you what, though, maybe I didn't like that, but I
respected it.

This is not your typical match, I know. Everything is at stake. Golf history is at stake. And probably more so for Tiger as it would turn out, but at the moment, I didn't appreciate all of that.

I'd rather have an opponent who is ice-cold and fierce than an obnoxious loudmouth who tries to get in your head—because his game lacks the ability to take care of business. No. This was just right. Your game does all the talking today, there's no beating around the bush; it's raw, unfiltered, and you're either ready or not. I respect that indeed. You know where each guy stands the whole time. Stares, swagger, and all.

Cue the Terminator music. Maybe I didn't see it at that moment, but the machine was indeed hiding under his white, soon-to-be red shirt, waiting to engage.

Somehow, the rest of those first 18 holes went much better than anticipated. We stuck to our game plan perfectly and *boom*, Steve is 5-up. I could not wait to get to the clubhouse and find a phone to call home. My family absolutely needed to stop what they're doing and watch!

Steve is killing Tiger right now!

I knew he could do it, but this was punishing—wow, just wow.

Steve put the brakes on my roll midway to the clubhouse; he knew this was like a false front on a tricky green. Nope. Five-up wasn't safe enough. Not by a mile.

I thought he was crazy, but I trusted him, so I simmered down. Dang it, I kept those emotions in check until I could get off the green, and now I gotta bottle them up again. Ugh.

Fine. Okay, maybe I'll squeeze out a little more excitement on the phone to my family, if they'd ever answer the dang phone!

Eventually, I got in touch with my family, who had been busy digging holes for fence posts (of all things); yes, they were going to turn on the TV at the start of the live coverage.

They could not believe Steve was doing so well!

Long lunch break, so long and quiet. We had lunch with Steve's Aunt Charlotte and Uncle Bill, and no one else was around, it seemed. Nice to be able to decompress, but not too much. Steve's game had been firing on all cylinders; we were like clockwork. Didn't want to spend the rest of the break time on the range or putting green—why? Our game is so on point. What is there to improve? Why spend time on the range? So you can let your perfectionist thoughts kidnap your game and hold it hostage for the next 18? Yes, you need to warm up again, but not be perfect. Steve was a feel player and not a "practicer." Much more akin to Ben Crenshaw than Tom Kite, although both are in the World Golf Hall of Fame and were taught the game by the legendary Harvey Penick.

So how to kill that time?

Shopping. A nice perk to having your girlfriend for a caddy!

A quick, and I mean speedy, time to shop for some souvenirs. I was so afraid to leave that course without some kind of Pumpkin Ridge item with the US Amateur logo on it. And for my family, too—since they couldn't be there. Matching IZOD shirts for both Steve and me—kind of corny, but sometimes we just were that way and still are to this day. And of course, a baseball hat with the giant US Amateur logo on it.

Back to business, roll up my sleeves and change gears.

DEEP DOWN, I WAS REALLY HOPING and slightly expecting Steve to just floor it from the first tee and on. End this match like no other—put Tiger so far down there was no hope left. Maybe that was my feet talking—long week—but I know it would be rather satisfactory to just make many jaws drop.

Eh.

Tiger changed his white shirt to red—which I thought was quite funny. Must have been careless at lunch and spilled something on the other. No, later I learn that is just his thing. The red shirt thing. The red shirt becomes his cape and wakes up the sleeping Tiger—good thing, because now the cameras are rolling.

Hole 7, which would be the 25th hole of our match, didn't seem all that tricky at first glance, but for some reason it was the layup where Steve would lose his focus. Maybe it wasn't a very demanding shot that took his focus away at times, but earlier in the week, on this hole I noted he needed a target for the layup—just a reinforcer to keep Steve focused on the shot at hand vs. the birdie putt his mind would already be on. This was the hole the NBC camera crew started to get in place, whether they were actually filming live or not. I got the butterflies in my stomach knowing we could be on television.

I wondered whether I should wave and say, "Hi!!" or just play it cool and smile.

Pretty sure I did both; we were on *TV.*

I knew Steve was way too zoned in to say hello, so I managed for both of us! A couple holes later, our match became a duel no one anticipated, but the world would never forget.

Steve's chip-in for birdie came on 10 (for which I went to give him a high five but ended up slapping his shoulder because he had skyrocketed to another planet with his victory jump), followed by the insane 11th hole, where Tiger rebounded like Shaq on the boards and answered back to Steve with his rollercoaster putt from across the world.

Nuts, these two.

No matter how much magic Tiger would pull out from under his sleeve, I had to remain unfazed. That is the other part of golf I appreciate: as much as you want to dance like Deion Sanders and celebrate great moments (I am a Florida girl, as you know), you can't, you just can't. You leave that up to the gallery. Especially when it's not in your favor. Trust me: if I could moonwalk across the green or MC Hammer it, I would have done that a few times that day on Steve's behalf.

It was the 12th hole, the 30th of this epic match, where suddenly I heard a few cheers from the crowd that were undeniably for Steve. As we were walking up to the 12th tee, the massive gallery was geez, ten-twelve deep by this time, at least?

That's when I made eye contact with some faces in the crowd, and they were cheering for my man, my honey. They appreciated what was happening and what was unfolding, too. We were not so alone anymore. We were picking up momentum more than I knew.

It's a moment forever etched in my mind as we were hunkering down. This guy, my guy, wasn't just gonna go down. There is no folding here. If Tiger had to perform miracles, then he was going to have to do just that—and that's exactly what it was going to take to beat Steve. Miracles. If Tiger had to walk on water to win today, I do believe he would have done just that.

Fine, then guess what. Well, don't expect that water to be smooth as glass, either. It is going to be choppy as hell.

Tidal waves, even.

As we continued and battled on, and weathered the storm of Tiger's amazing comeback, the cheers for Steve grew.

Like an incoming tide chasing a full moon, they grew.

I remember walking off the 14th green, our 32nd hole of the match, and even more people from the gallery would holler and tell me they were rooting for us, looking me in the eye. The energy was buzzing all over the place; the support from the gallery was like getting sprinkled with fairy dust by Tinkerbell herself, to where the bag started feeling lighter and lighter. Cameras following our every move, the crowd continued to grow—how easy it would be to get lost in all of it.

It's surreal to be in that moment, and it's like you're in a bubble, where it's quiet, calm, and crystal clear in front of you, but hazy everywhere else. The day itself was a gorgeous day. I bet not even a cloud in the sky—I know I looked up, but I honestly can't remember exactly what I saw.

There were moments where time felt like it stood still, a statue, the Lincoln Memorial, me in Abraham's high-backed chair, and a breeze would brush my face and I could take this all in, and other times where the only people out there were me and Steve, Tiger and Brian. Certain holes I remember that bubble a bit more, like walking down that 14th fairway, one of Steve's favorite holes at Pumpkin Ridge.

During stroke play, on 14, Steve hit this ridiculous recovery shot over a tree to the right of the green. Steve tends to have quite a few ridiculous shots per round; I guess I just expect them and take them for granted. Though I probably shouldn't, as his caddy.

Steve and I would walk down that fairway, and it was a moment where the energy needed a pause, just a breather, so we would talk about the TV crane we'd often see in the distance, remembering how he kept hitting that darn thing a year ago at the US Amateur in Rhode Island.

We used it for wind direction; the flag would wave to let us know where the predominant wind was. I also remember chanting to Steve that he was the *man*—he's got this. And he'd have that tough-guy look in his eye with a fierce "Yeah!" without the words, on our way to the green.

I also like to lighten up the moments on the green from time to time; started this when I caddied at the US Open for Steve a couple months prior. We would talk to his ball and tell it to go in the hole. Very childlike and corny, I know. But that was us. Childlike and corny. I love to be silly, and to bring the silly out of others, and sometimes it's my way of deflecting pressure. Smiles and laughs go a long way toward releasing negative, stressful energy. Movie lines, too, and Steve knows *Caddyshack* way too well.

Match play is a marathon, not a sprint. And in match play, it's not the total score. It's about focus, and just beating the guy you are facing like your reflection in a mirror, by one shot on each hole. One shot—that's all it takes. Makes you stay in the present. So, if silly keeps you in the present, then whatever it takes, it takes.

So we find ourselves on 16, the 34th hole of this insanely epic match, and the freaking bunker on the right got Steve again. But he is so great with bunker shots. The way he's playing, I truly thought he could hole it.

But it was fate, wasn't it?

The whole ball mark situation. *Hey, Tiger—did you move that back?*

Steve makes his putt, and just as second nature as it is to acknowledge a good shot, it's second nature to him to remind Tiger to move his mark back. I think nothing of it. Clueless of the gravity of it, that if Steve stays silent, we win the US Amateur right then and there, my mind is moving onto the next hole—we're running out of holes to put this Tiger guy away.

Funny, to replaying that hole in my mind today, I think about how in that very moment, Steve's true character shines brighter than the sun that day. No pause, no recognition, no dramatic show-stopping theatrics to announce what just took place. Just so matter-of-fact. A fleeting moment that is timeless.

We move on and just keep going, but Tiger keeps pulling putts out of his you know what.

Tiger truly is amazing. I have to say that. You've got to give credit where credit is due.

We are so close to the finish line, and though the nerves are doing their best to test Steve's last one, he prevails on the 18th, our 36th, sending this finals US Amateur round into sudden death.

Sudden Death.

Another long wait— had to be on the first hole of sudden death, didn't it? The hole where there is a huge advantage to Tiger. Hole number 9.

We make our way to the tee, and there is a wait. Like a visit to the doctor's office kind of wait, with the lobby empty and you are the last patient but still you wait for ages. Minutes hang on the walls of your "Let's go!" emotions like bats in a cave.

An uncomfortable amount of time we had to wait, but I use it to my advantage, or at least I try to. A loving, supportive massage to the broad shoulders of my man where tension loves to store itself.

Steve needs the human touch right now before having to gather up the reserves of focus he has left. He needs that one last moment of support and undeniable belief that he has got this—to keep doing his thing, to know that he's the man, that he's destined to be here at this moment in time and prevail.

This is not Tiger's day; this is *Steve's* day.

TALKING ABOUT THE TARGET, REINFORCING THE SWING thought that has worked all week, all day, and will continue to do so for this shot and the shot after it. Finish to the target. That's it.

Just finish to the target. Just a stock, solid swing, and finish to the target.

Nothing heroic. Steve could do this blindfolded.

Perfect tee shot—just nails it. Approach shot, and we're first, with a 5-iron in. Tiger is in the fairway with a wedge in hand. Doesn't matter that the distance advantage is on Tiger's side, because Steve rifles that 5-iron like it was a wedge and sticks it closer than Tiger.

In your face! is what I think to myself.

Steve's beloved putter was hot so much this week, but on this putt to win it all, it just would not be, leaving the door open for one more playoff hole. Dang it. Just dang it.

But it's okay, it's okay, it's all okay. Because we're going to a hole Steve has the better memory from. From the morning match, I mean. The 10th, where he chipped in that epic flop shot, and we also learned he had some rockets in his shoes, like Iron Man, right before he shoots off into the sky.

I searched high and low for a positive, and that was an easy one. I know Steve was pissed at himself for not draining that putt, but that slap on the shoulder from me would shut off those thoughts the best I could shut them out. It's a loving slap . . . like slap tap . . . you know what I mean? What I wanted to do was take him by his imaginary helmet and slam it into my imaginary helmet and say, "You got this, one more hole, this is your hole . . . now which club are you gonna use? But I had to do such without the helmet.

Yeah, I was a big football fan then.

Okay, number 10. We've got you this time, Tiger. Steve's not going to miss this in the rough like last time, he's got his target. Darn flag is on the right, though—no matter, this is Steve's hole.

Steve hits his shot, and it doesn't draw in quite enough and it's in the rough. Again. Dang it.

But Tiger's shot isn't a gimme, either.

I remember reminding Steve about his incredible pitch from the last time we were here and saying how he knows just what to do—he still has that advantage as we're walking toward the green.

This would've been a good time for a movie line, but I was too focused on finding the positives for a pitch shot that was, truthfully, a very tough shot. A really tough shot to get close. But what Steve did impeccably well for these shots was use his imagination; he could picture just how it should fly, where it should land and roll into the hole. All week, Steve could sense the thickness of the rough in his hands when he took practice swings, and how open or closed he wanted that clubface to be, this angle or that, the length of his swing, how shallow or steep his swing needed to be, how much tension he needed in his grip, how wide his stance needed to be, and how much flexion his knees would need.

All this computing done at a computer's pace, easy calculations for Steve under normal circumstances; but this time victory was within reach, and the pressure insurmountable.

I watch Steve like a hawk. His tempo and his swing looked the same, his practice routine looked the same. This was his bread and butter. His eyes stared down that flag like they had all day, his swagger told me all I needed to know. That's what I needed to see, and perhaps I could exhale, just a little.

There was no doubt in my mind this was going to be a great shot.

As Steve settled in and waggled moments before he started his backswing, I could hardly look (the tension was so intense I could have exploded!) —but I did look—and damn, that ball *just* missed holing out again!

I had immediate tears in my eyes, just so proud he came that close. Only titanium insides can produce that shot at that moment. Good God, how did he manage to swing that club with just the right touch . . . again . . . with the match, the entire tournament, on the line? Man, did he give that all he had.

Sadly, Steve missed the comeback putt to put extra pressure on Tiger to make, and in a blink of an eye, maybe four blinks—mine, and Steve's both—with Tiger's tap-in from one foot away, it was over.

That was it. No miraculous shot to conquer Steve. A darn tap-in.

But.

Just a phenomenal comeback from Tiger. There is no denying that.

You have to give credit where credit is due, even when it doesn't fall on you.

THE 15,000-PLUS CROWD GOES WILD WHEN TIGER'S putt drops, and we retreat to our neutral corner, so to speak, the back right part of the green if memory serves, awaiting what the next steps are.

Roger Maltbie, the legendary commentator (Roger really is special—he is so good at saying all the right things at all the right times) asks us if Tiger has shaken Steve's hand as time winds on. I think Roger asked knowing we/Steve and Tiger hadn't.

Man, that was awkward.

Felt like we were in the way of Tiger's celebration, honestly. I may have asked Roger what should we do? Should we stay on the green or leave? Steve and I looked at each other not really knowing what the right thing to do was. Understandably, of course, Tiger would hug his parents—can't remember if his entire entourage was also hugged—but with the time we were standing there, it felt like he hugged everyone in the crowd.

Steve and Tiger did eventually shake hands, but I can't remember at what point.

Maybe prior to his TV interview?

MY FINAL MEMORY OF PUMPKIN RIDGE and that unbelievable day was the trophy presentation.

Judy Bell, the USGA president at the time (I remember, because it was historic for a female to be president), said many great things about the match and acknowledged Steve for his play that day—who couldn't? Steve, in turn, was sure to thank the Pumpkin Ridge Golf Club, and the USGA, for a great event and of course gave many praises and congratulations to Tiger. Steve and I were equally blown away with what took place out there.

But then Tiger's turn came, and his speech didn't mention Steve. Not in the least. As in not at all.

And that really bothered me.

Seriously, Tiger? How many hours were we out there? Steve

didn't lay down and hand you the match; you had to earn that trophy harder than you ever have in the past. And it was too tough to show your opponent the respect he deserved?

Maybe Tiger didn't know Steve, and certainly did know *of* him, but you can at least acknowledge an awesome duel in the sun when it happens.

So no, I didn't leave that day with the impression that the guy holding the trophy valued the traditions of golf. The lack of respect that was given to Steve is one of the basic traditions that Tiger shunned. Maybe it was just an oversight, a simple one—oops. The moment took Tiger by the tail, perhaps. But as I added the tally I'd been keeping in my head that day, it painted a different impression than the Monet I wanted to remember.

I know I probably sound pretty negative about someone who would become one of the most influential figures this game of golf will ever know. Tiger changed the game of golf forever in so many ways, single-handedly.

Maybe I'm expecting too much in such a moment as this.

Over time, my first impression, as sour as it grew, would watch Tiger evolve and hope I was wrong. And what does it matter, really, my opinion? The thing is, it doesn't. I met Tiger on an extraordinary day, in an extraordinary match, under extraordinary conditions. I had no way of knowing that he wasn't brought up with the same values Steve and I shared. Tiger was brought up to become a machine. To understand and rewrite golf's history, perhaps, but he had a job to do, and that was winning *every single thing* he ever played in.

Growing up that way, you miss out on the beautiful journey this game brings, each different to everyone. But those who play and appreciate the game of golf the most have a love for the game of golf that is beyond trophies, hardware, and million-dollar checks. And when you're training to become a machine, perhaps that journey is a mere mission: you seek and destroy vs. absorbing what golf wants to teach you. Life lessons and values, all while you walk on grass and greens and fairways and rough and hit a ball around some incredible settings, if you're lucky.

What is the first rule in golf?

Integrity.

Respect for your playing partners, the course, and the rules of the game.

What other sport has *that* as its first rule?

None. Because no other sport requires the players to be their own referees.

This is engrained in me, and we know it was engrained in Steve as he showed the world on the 34th hole of that epic match. The gravity of Steve not being a machine that day is why the match ended the way it did.

Asking Tiger to move his mark back is what golf taught Steve to do, subconsciously, innately. The values of the game and life run through his veins, thicker than blood I'd say, and knowing that historic moment is a lesson for all to learn from makes me most proud.

Steve Scott preserved the game of golf forever, in a thankless moment.

It may have been too hard for Tiger to shake Steve's hand or give him a nod with words, at least at that moment in time. And maybe, too, Tiger needed 20 years to go by to finally give credit where credit was due; maybe he too needed to process that day, decades later, to fully appreciate what it was, in different terms. And to this day (in Tiger's words, not mine), he always marks his ball with the coin heads up. If he ever has to move it, he flips it over to tails, to remind him to move it back. Tiger called what Steve did a testament to what the game is all about.

Perhaps Tiger is human after all.

ACKNOWLEDGMENTS

To EVEN BEGIN TO THINK ABOUT THE lengthy list of people who have helped me in my life might actually be longer than this entire book, so I will keep this as short and sweet as I can, but I wanted to make sure to single out a few key people who have meant so much to me over the years for various reasons. Because there are too many to name all of you, please know whether I have listed you in this book or I haven't, in my heart of hearts your words, actions, guidance, and love (no matter the amount) has truly had a profound impact in my 43+ years on this Earth. So many chance encounters and life situations along the way have shaped my being for the better, and whether each individual I have encountered in my life knows it or not, you have made me appreciate each and every moment and not take a second for granted.

So, first I say thank you to each one of my friends, class-mates, coaches, teachers, teammates, opponents, sponsors, golfing buddies, doctors, neighbors, bosses, fellow PGA Professionals, and former assistant pros for playing an impactful role in my life. For those who taught me for free and helped a middle-class kid play a rich man's sport on a budget, I will forever be indebted to you, and I hope you know who you are.

To the unselfish mentors, teachers, and coaches I had in the game who gave me their time and their words of wisdom over the years to shape my homemade golf swing and golfing mind. I'm forever indebted to my first coach, Ray Daley, for paying it forward and seeing the potential in a young kid with a ten-finger grip. To my high school coaches Bob Schmidt, Wally Dunne, and Marilyn Rule for guiding us to a couple of state titles and my coach at the University of Florida, Buddy Alexander, for helping my family with a full scholarship and me with my mind—there was a lot to work on! To Bob Ford for always picking up my calls late at night and for your never-ending wisdom. Having the chance to caddie for two seasons at Seminole for the likes of Jack Nicklaus, Gary Player, Lanny Wadkins, and Jimmy Dunne was a lasting memory I will always take with me. Bob, I will always wonder what it would've been like to work for you at Oakmont.

Thanks, Bob Toski, for never charging me a dime for a lesson even though those lessons were worth their weight in gold. I'll never forget our daylong sessions on the back of your range at BCC—you always held court and you were the judge, the jury, and the executioner! To Michael Breed, Martin Hall, Bill Davis, and Mike Adams, thank you for sharing and caring for my game and well-being. Your understanding of the game is remarkable, and your continued thirst for knowledge, combined with your passion and enthusiasm, rubs off on everyone you know. Thank you for all of your contributions.

Although your opponents can't directly impact your score in the individual sport of golf, they can push you to work harder and climb to higher heights. Thanks to my longtime friend

Robert Hooper for also being my first memorable adversary in the game. Starting when we were about twelve, we played all the time whether it was for fun at Eagle Trace (thank you and your family for always having me as your guest!) or in a tournament at PGA National or the Naples Beach Club. I was always in awe of your golf swing and game (still am), and you no doubt pushed me to become a tougher competitor in our formative years. We were teammates in both high school and college and were groomsmen in each other's weddings. Although we wanted to beat each other's brains in, if one of us couldn't win we always pulled for each other, and I appreciate our friendship to this day.

Thanks, Hoops.

It's AMAZING AS YOU GO THROUGH LIFE you never know who you might meet that will set your life truly in motion. A big thank-you has to go to Amy Spooner (Johnston) for hooking up that group bowling date with Kristi and me way back in November 1994. If not for you, I never would've run into her in that mall parking lot that day, and Team Scott never happens. I have to say that going all the way back to high school, I admired your courage to overcome a crushing defeat in the state championship on a technicality to go on to capture a monumental USGA championship: the U.S. Amateur Public Links. I'll forever be envious of your attitude, perseverance, and outlook on life. Thank you for always being a friend.

Following my playing days as I moved into the PGA Professional ranks, there were so many people who gave me the opportunity to develop in the country club scene to become a complete golf professional. Outside of the tournament play, I wanted to be a great instructor, a merchandiser, a mentor, and a leader. Several friends and leaders passed along their knowledge and gave me a chance to grow in the business. Thanks to Donny Lee and Dave Maga at the Golf Digest Schools, my first boss at a private club in Greg Lecker at Canoe Brook, and Ian Dalzell for always making going to work fun at Hidden Creek and Brian Boushie for guiding me as a golf professional at Jupiter Hills. Many thanks to Joel and Pam Moore for giving me my very first head professional position at The Ridge at Back Brook. What a private enclave you created there in the New Jersey farmland! Tremendous appreciation to Jeff Mandelbaum and family as well as Steve Lapper, who gave me the reigns at Paramount Country Club. You gave my family and me one of the greatest gifts to live on property and serve as the golf professional at your fine club in the Metropolitan PGA Section for six years. You gave me the freedom to compete in tournaments and grow my broadcasting career, as well. I will forever be grateful for your kindness to my family, and I hope we never lose touch.

To Will Smith, Quentin Lutz, Colin Sheehan, Chris Hunt, and the entire team at my current-day position with the Outpost Club and Silver Club Golfing Society, thank you for creating a group of true golfers with the deepest respect for the game and its holding true to its traditions. To have this opportunity for our family to move near Kristi's parents in North Carolina has been a tremendous blessing. In this business as a PGA Professional, it's almost impossible to find the perfect club and job in the ideal area of the country that is also near family. I hit a home run with you all, and I'm honored to be on a great team with people who have fully mastered the meaningful aspects of a camaraderie-filled, thriving golfing society.

I must give a shoutout to the people who have given me

some wonderful opportunities to continue to develop in the golf broadcasting and media space. Thanks to Barry Hyde, Mark Loomis, Pat Leahy, and Greg Hopfe for seeing my potential and passion I have for connecting the golf fans more deeply to the game as an analyst and instructor. It's been awesome to be able to call shots for some of the best players to ever play the game and help everyone learn to play the game better.

I HONESTLY NEVER THOUGHT I WOULD EVER WRITE A BOOK. No way. Too long and tedious an exercise, or so I thought. Tripp Bowden (in addition to Skyhorse Publishing and our great editor, Julie Ganz), I have to sincerely thank you during this journey as my cowriter, for your passion, vision, and belief in this story. Without a doubt, if we don't meet at the exact time that we did in December 2019, this book simply doesn't exist. Our chance encounter through The Outpost Club and Silver Club Golfing Society continued to show me that every moment in life is purposeful and every person we encounter in life is a potential friend guiding you toward your next mission or passion in life. As we dived into this process, it completely blew my mind how much you helped uncover and make clear once again all the memories I had locked inside for all of these years. Tripp, you and I were meant to cross paths exactly when we did and I will always be appreciative of this time in our lives when, together, we captured this moment in history for the next generations to forever understand how to embody the true spirit of the game of golf (and life).

As far as family goes, Dad, I can never thank you enough for introducing me to this game of a lifetime and instilling love and support while never pushing me. Without you getting me into the game and teaching me right from wrong at such a young age, this story never gets told. Instinctively, I would never have known to look Tiger's way on that 34th hole. Even though you weren't physically in Portland on that final day, you were there within me. You simply guided me down the path I took, always driving me to this tournament or that tournament. Taking me to see Ray all those Saturday mornings like you did. I will never forget our times together on the golf course, especially our epic trip to Cypress Point and Pebble Beach. I know you always joked that I got my talents from somewhere.

Well, yes, I did.

Thanks also to Aunt Charlotte and my late Uncle Bill for your unwavering generosity and walking each and every step at Pumpkin Ridge with us. If not for you, Kristi wouldn't have made the trip, and very likely this whole story unfolds differently. After my opening round 79, I'm sure you probably thought we'd be making that trip back to Florida pretty quickly, but as every day went by, although your feet got more and more tired, the excitement grew and so did my appreciation for each of you. Kristi and I will never ever forget that week with you, and we'll never be able to thank you enough. Big thanks also to Wayne and Debbie for always supporting through these great times at all of my events. It meant a lot for you to be there in those memorable moments.

To my mom and stepdad, even though you/we moved all over the place, I'll never forget those good times in Arkansas and Memphis that helped shape me into the man I am today. Having the chance to get to meet Tom Kite in his prime in the early '90s and Greg Norman through your connections at the radio stations will be something I'll always treasure. And winning the dance contest to "Ice Ice Baby" in 8th grade was pretty cool. I know somewhere Grandpa and Grandma are looking down and smiling, too, and I know they both had a hand in where I am today. I will always appreciate your love and support, and my sweet tooth will forever be grateful for the sugary treats you'd always make.

To my brother, Roger, for always including me in your front-yard football games with the neighbors and teaching me to be a competitive little brother. You're the one who really sparked my fire in sports even though I didn't realize it at a young age, but I definitely do now. Even though you're more than five years my senior, you never treated me as such. I always felt your love and involvement, and I know you would go to the ends of the Earth to see me play a tournament or for whatever, and often you actually did. Thanks to you and Julie for everything, and may you continue to chase your dreams.

To my in-laws, Jeff and Kaye, I will always be thankful for your welcoming me into your "Farkel" family like I was one of yours. Your love, support, and generosity will always be something that I hope to reciprocate. You raised your beautiful Kristi to be strong and independent and taught her all the values that a great mother (and caddy) should have. Thank you for helping to create "Team Scott" and being there for our family at every turn. Thanks also to Kim, Daniel, Mikki, Brian, John, AJ, and Jimmy for your support over the years. The lengths that you all have gone to for family are simply amazing, and I also have to put "GG" and "Ba" on the same pedestal.

Selfless people don't come around too often in the world, and I am thankful to have you in my life.

Most important, to my loving wife, Kristi, and my two children, J.C. and Kaylie. Honey, ever since we held hands for the first time and shared that cinnamon pretzel at the mall, we were simply meant to be. Less than a month into dating, the word "like" just didn't cut it, and it didn't take long to know that you were my everything. And that was just our senior year of high school. You always believed in my game, and as a caddy you never let me give up. I can still feel those timely back massages when you could sense I was getting nervous. With zero sports psychologist training, you never let my mind waver in the most key moments and were always there to distract me if you felt I was getting too down on myself. Your timing was uncanny, and your instincts as a caddy surpassed my greatest expectations. Whether you were wearing the normal caddy bib or the full-out white jumpsuit at Augusta, you were always right there saying or doing the right thing (and looking pretty hot doing it, I might add), and I'm picky. I can't believe we have had so many surreal experiences in life at such a young age, both on and off the golf course. Marrying you two days before my 22nd birthday was one of the single best days of my life. The other two greatest days to compare to our wedding day were when our J.C. and Kaylie came into the world. I couldn't even begin to imagine spending my life with anyone but you.

You are this family's rock, the greatest wife and mother that anybody could ask for, and I will love you for the next thousand lifetimes.

J.C. and Kaylie, the love I have for you will equally never go away, even when I'm not around anymore to hug and kiss you goodnight. As I write this, I'm envisioning the future when I've moved on from this life and you are reading this story to your grandkids, or maybe they're reading it to their own grandkids 100 years from now. One of the most important human fundamentals I want to pass along to you with this story is to always make sure that you treat your opponents or your teammates with the same level of respect and decency. If they do something great, congratulate them. If you see them about to break a rule, let them know. Help them. You should battle hard and never give up, but at the same time always trust the moral compass instilled by your mom and me and don't *ever* put victory in front of performing as an honorable competitor. Win fairly and honestly. Win with class. Lose with dignity. Act unselfishly. Always hold your head high, no matter the outcome. Show respect to the game or the situation. If you follow your heart and your gut using these tenets as your guides, you will never go wrong. And when you finish whatever it is that you set out to do, know that you gave it your best and if your best wasn't good enough that day, you can always sleep well at night knowing that you left everything you had in that moment. Whether it be in golf, in school, in business, or with your own family someday, give it your 100 percent best and never look back. That is the most important life lesson I can ever share with you. I could never be prouder about anything in my life than I am about you both, and I know you will continue to achieve great things in life.

In closing, I want to acknowledge you, the reader of this book. Thank you for your time to take in an important piece of golf history and fully grasp the spirit of the game. Coming to the realization that holding the trophy at the very end doesn't necessarily render you the true victor is not easy to comprehend in today's society, but it's an important epiphany to have. I hope reading this book has given you a greater appreciation for not only *why* we play the game, but *how* to play the game. My only wish for everyone who reads this book is that you pay this story forward. Pass it along to the next generations who will follow in your footsteps. Go through life knowing that your actions are powerful and every word you say can literally change the course of history. Because when you live your life ethically and without regret, you never lose sleep about what might have been. The pressures of the past or the anxieties of the future fade away. Rather than consuming yourself in outcomes, engulf yourself in the journey that life takes us on, because even in defeat, it's all positive if you perceive it as such. If you can manage to navigate your time on Earth in this manner, at that point you will understand what I've realized for the last 9,000-plus days, or almost 25 years since that magical day on August 25, 1996.

That you can actually win in life without winning. I think I'm walking proof of that.

Steven Marshall Scott
February 8, 2021

ACKNOWLEDGMENTS PART II

STEVE SAID IT BEST, BUT I WOULD like to say a few bests, as well.

To thank folks after you have written a book, man, what a task, yet what a beautiful problem to have. Who to leave in, who to leave out? It's like making up your wedding guest list: once you get started, you go for days, and next thing you know you have five hundred people showing up at the church and of course they are more than welcome, but how the heck are you are gonna feed 'em and give 'em something to wash the eats down with?

So—I truly am gonna keep it simple, best as I can.

To Julie Ganz, my amazing editor, who believes in me and my story lines, and puts up with and makes sense of my rabbit hole self, and knows just when to rein me in and when to let me run like a wild-ass mustang through the wide-open prairie fields of storyland.

You are the best, Julie. Thank you.

To Skyhorse Publishing, thank you for opening the door once again to an absolutely incredible story. Thank you, Tony, the design team, publication team, marketing team, et al.

To my incredible bride of twenty-three years, Fletch, who believes in me even in times when I have given her proof there is no need to, I thank you for loving me unconditionally.

To our amazing kiddos, Arrie B and Holly Mac. Okay, I'm gonna call you out. Y'all really are some kind of special. Don't let it go to your heads. Squads could not be prouder of you than he is of himself.

HAHA!

I know you get that joke.

To Pop and Cissy, thank you for loving me, and for the feedback on Fripp Island, New Year's Day, 2021. You were right. I needed to do better, and thanks to you, I did.

To Mum and Peter, thank you for reading the manuscript when it was raw as store-bought bacon and encouraging me like crazy during COVID-19, even though my writing, at the time, was more akin to *burnt* store-bought bacon.

And, of course, for loving me.

To my dear cousin, Kathy, a.k.a. Cuz, who read this book *super* raw, like sushi, and gave me some ethereal thoughts on how to cook it. Thank you, thank you, thank you.

And to the impeccable Pat Conroy, whose brilliant writing I always read when I'm trying to put my best pen to paper and challenge the storyteller in me to be so much better than I really am.

It always works.

You should try it sometime.

My last thank-you is to Steve and Kristi Scott.

Steve, if you hadn't sat directly to the left of me at that dinner table at Champions Retreat and told me, quite casually I might add, as if you were asking me to pass you the butter, that you had asked Tiger to move his mark back and I went HOLY MOLY.

The whole table erupted, and my writing brain exploded. Not sure if it was the left side or right—I can never remember which side is the creative side of the ol' encephalon.

Well, if not for that meant-to-be-moment-in-time on that stars-aligned December night in 2019, none of this happens.

I'm glad it happened.

Man, am I ever. And to think this train is just starting to roll. I can't wait to see where she takes us.

Thank you, Steve, and Kristi, for opening up your hearts to me during the telling of this beautiful story. I know it wasn't always easy.

PLAY THE GAME THE RIGHT WAY, Y'ALL. Play the game like Steve.

Tripp Bowden
February 8, 2021